TABLE OF CONTENTS

ACKNOWLEDGMENTS

YALSA IS DEEPLY grateful to the contributors who helped make this book possible; your guidance on summer reading and advice on a variety of topics will help guide teen library staff for years to come. Thanks to Mark Flowers, Megan Honig, Erin Downey Howerton, Kat Kan, Maria Kramer, Chris Shoemaker, and Connie Urquhart for their hard work.

In addition, this book is supported by a Carnegie-Whitney Award from the American Library Association. Our thanks to ALA's Publications Committee for its long-standing support of YALSA's publishing initiatives.

INTRODUCTION

IN 2010, AUTHOR David Von Drehle argued in *Time* that the summer break between school years did a near-insurmountable amount of damage to the achievement of American youth in grades K–12, particularly among low-income students:

> "Call it 'summer learning loss,' as the academics do, or 'the summer slide,' but by any name summer vacation is among the most pernicious—if least acknowledged—causes of achievement gaps in America's schools," von Drehle argued. "…By the time the bell rings on a new school year, the poorer kids have fallen weeks, if not months behind. And even well-off American students may be falling behind their peers around the world."[1]

Earlier that summer, Dominican University released a report, written as part of an Institute of Museum and Library Services–funded grant, on the effect that public library summer reading programs had on closing the achievement gap and improving reading skill levels among school-aged youth. One way to close that reading gap, the researchers found, is to support summer reading at the library. The Dominican Report's chief finding indicated that "[s]tudents who participated in the public library summer reading program scored higher on reading achievement tests at the beginning of the next school year than those students who did not participate and they gained in other ways as well."[2] The study collected data from eleven sites across the United States and found that students who participated in library summer reading programs scored higher on reading achievement tests than those who did not and came back to school ready to learn, with improved reading comprehension skills and more confidence in addition to their improved test scores.

Recognizing this important role, libraries have hosted summer reading programs for more than 100 years, welcoming children, tweens, and teens into their stacks and meeting rooms for book discussions and activities designed to broaden horizons. Summer reading programs are a routine part of any library's schedule, with hundreds of hours and significant budget dollars devoted to them. In addition to educating youth, they offer libraries a chance to boost their own presence within a community, simply by becoming more visible to patrons and readers or by engaging in significant partnerships with local businesses or like-minded organizations.

But there are few guidebooks out there to help plan a summer library reading program, particularly one focusted on tweens and teens ages 12-18. This is where *YALSA's Complete Summer Reading Manual* comes in. While many libraries do use resources from the Collaborative Summer Library Program, its content is not focused on the unique needs and interests of those ages 12-18, whereas the content of this book is written expressly for those who work with that age group. In addition to providing activity ideas and sample reading incentive programs, this book offers a roadmap for teen library specialists charged with planning summer reading, from budgeting to evaluation, including marketing the summer reading program, creating partnerships with community organizations and local businesses, incorporating technology, and finding tools and sources for effective readers' advisory. Advice and sample programs have been collated from multiple organizations across the United States, ensuring tips and tools for libraries of any type and any budget. To round out the advice, enjoy additional articles with tips on devising fun games and food-based activities, bringing in volunteers, reaching special populations, and developing no-cost programs.

Library staff can use this resource to plan effective programs and ensure that youth in their community keep their reading skills active over the summer and do not experience the "boredom, inactivity, and isolation" that von Drehle cautions against in his polemic.[3] But they can also make sure that the teens have a little fun while they're maintaining their skills.

REFERENCES

1. Von Drehle, David. "The Case Against Summer Vacation," *Time* 176, no. 5 (2010): 36.
2. Dominican University. "The Dominican Study: Public Library Summer Reading Programs Close the Reading Gap," June 2010, http://www.dom.edu/gslis/downloads/DOM_IMLS_executiveSummary.pdf (accessed May 22, 2012).
3. Von Drehle, "The Case Against Summer Vacation," 36.

Planning and Budgeting

Connie Urquhart

BEHIND EVERY HIT summer reading program (SRP) lies an autumn, winter, and spring of meticulous planning. While teens may be aware of the program only during summer, a team of librarians are working year-round to ensure its success. The process can seem daunting from the outset, but is much more manageable when broken down into parts. This chapter will examine each stage of the planning process as follows:

1. Staffing
2. Goals and Objectives
3. Program Components
4. Budget and Fundraising
5. Developing a Timeline

Staffing

The first step in building a top-notch SRP is putting together a top-notch team. Even in smaller libraries where staff is in short supply, it is always necessary to identify key people who may have talent, experience, or a unique perspective to contribute—whether or not they are paid employees. Who are the stakeholders? Who can offer time, expertise, and knowledge? People in this group may include other library staff, teachers, community partners, or teens themselves. It may also be beneficial to identify people working on a children's summer reading program and explore how the two teams can pool resources for maximum efficacy.

While it's not necessary to define clearly the size and scale of the program just yet, it is important to have a ballpark figure of how many people it will take to get the job done. If a large group is assembled, it is smart to appoint several people to lead subcommittees. This assigns specific people primary responsibility to such areas as incentives, programs, and marketing while freeing up the SRP coordinator to keep track of the big picture. The majority of work can be accomplished from remote locations, so team members need not meet as regularly as might have been necessary in the past. The team leaders should remember that by utilizing online work spaces and conducting virtual meetings, they may be able to recruit help from staff in remote branches or community partners whose availability is limited to evenings.

That said, there are times when face-to-face meetings are ideal. The first meeting is a good time to establish the program's goals and objectives (described in the next section), which usually requires a healthy discussion. There are other times when brainstorming is necessary, and in-person meetings generally foster an environment that allows people to build off of each other's ideas. Personalities and work approaches differ and each person or team will find what works best for their own needs. Setting clearly defined expectations and deadlines will help, as will open lines of communication between the committee members, SRP coordinator, and library administration.

Finally, a word about staffing during the actual SRP. It is crucial for the planning team to keep in mind the human resources necessary to implement the program. This could mean paid employees, volunteers (both adult and teen), Friends of the Library, or any combination thereof. Knowing how many bodies or hours will be available during the summer will help keep the planning process on track. Aiming high can produce fantastic results, but creating a program that is impossible to implement given the available resources isn't realistic. It is the planning team's responsibility to find a balance.

Goals and Objectives

Why have a teen summer reading program? The reasons may seem obvious, but articulating the goals for the library's SRP is critical. Having specific goals and objectives in place will prove helpful when making every kind of decision, from budgeting to scheduling to marketing. It will also help convince potential funders why they should donate to such a valuable program.

First, the team should choose a few goals they would like to see met during the course of the summer. They might also set longer-term goals, in which they see progress over several years. Goals should be achievable given the library's resources, but they should also strive for an improved reality at the finish. They should be broad in scope and support the very general, overarching mission statement of the organization.

To identify goals, the team should try answering questions such as:

- How can teens benefit from participating?
- How can the library benefit?
- What potential community partnerships can be fostered?

Answering those questions will make it easier for goals to take shape. Examples of teen SRP goals could be:

- To encourage reading for pleasure
- To transition tweens from the children's SRP program into year-round offerings for teens
- To help guide older teens toward the library's resources for adults
- To establish a positive relationship between teens and the library
- To attract and introduce new patrons to the library's resources
- To demonstrate to teens the library's dedication to technology
- To engage teens' minds while they are away from school
- To provide a beneficial way to engage community youth
- To create or strengthen the relationship between area schools and public library
- To recruit teen volunteers for help during the school year

All of the examples listed above won't be appropriate for every library, so it is important that when identifying goals they reflect the specific needs of the community. The planning team should look at what makes their population unique, and discuss all the special challenges this group presents. Those challenges are the key to establishing the program's goals.

Once goals have been identified, the next step is setting objectives. Objectives are tangible, quantifiable outcomes that are used to measure whether or not the goals have been met. Figure 1.1 shows goals on the left with possible objectives to the right. It is common to have several objectives per goal.

The planning team should remember that the means with which a mission is achieved may not be direct. For example, if a library's mission is to increase literacy, it behooves the team to keep an open mind about how to achieve this goal. During the summer of 2011, Ann Arbor District Library in Michigan de-emphasized reading by creating an online game called Summer Game 2011. Players earned points for completing a variety of tasks, from reading to attending events to requesting an item using the online catalog. The points were added to the game's leaderboard and could be redeemed for prizes based on point value. They found that by creating a more holistic experience, reading levels actually increased from previous years.

The success of Ann Arbor and other libraries' unconventional summer programs is an excellent reminder to keep an open mind regarding the planning team's own program. If the sample goals listed here can be

Goal	Objective
To encourage reading for pleasure	Booktalk at least one book per genre (including formats such as magazines, graphic novels, nonfiction, or online articles) while promoting the SRP to teens
To establish a positive relationship between teens and the library	Include teens in the planning process, especially regarding events and prizes
To demonstrate to teens the library's dedication to technology	Incorporate technology into at least 60 percent of programs
To recruit teen volunteers for help during the school year	Offer volunteering as a way to earn prizes during the SRP

FIGURE 1.1. Sample Goals and Objectives.

achieved more effectively using an outside-the-box approach, why not consider different program elements? The next section will focus on suggested components, but how the team chooses to execute the components is limited only to each member's imagination.

Program Components

The planning team has been identified; goals and objectives have been set. After establishing the duration and the dates that the SRP will span, it's time to determine which elements to incorporate into the program. The first step is reading the evaluations from last year's program. What worked and what didn't? What did teens and staff like, and what did they think was missing?

If the planning team does not include teens, now is the time to bring them aboard. Many of the following components' success hinge upon the teens in the library's particular community. What works in one place might not work in another. If the library already has a teen advisory board, this is the perfect time to get their input. If not, consider advertising for a teen focus group off of which to bounce ideas. They may save the planning team from heading in a wayward direction, and no one knows other teens better then their peers.

A teen SRP's components might include the following areas.

THEME

While most SRPs have a theme, the ways in which a theme is chosen can vary. The team may decide to go with their own theme. This allows for maximum creativity and the opportunity to tailor the theme to the library's community. However, this also means creating a logo, graphics, and all marketing materials. If the team decides to use a theme chosen by a local or national consortium, much of the prep work is already done. Where customization is sacrificed, the trade off is the opportunity to purchase ready-to-go posters, reading logs, t-shirts, and more. Whether the team decides to use their own theme or that of a consortium, they may want to consider pairing with the children's SRP planning team. Having just one theme for the entire library means less time and money in the creation or purchasing of graphics and marketing materials.

PARTICIPATION TRACKING

The most traditional way that libraries track participation is via reading logs. Logs are usually paper but they could have an online counterpart, and the way in which reading is counted can vary as well: pages, whole books, or length of time spent reading. In addition, some libraries choose to offer participation credit for activities other than reading. This could include any of the following: submitting book reviews; volunteering; attending library events; interacting with the library's website or social media outlets; playing games that teach information literacy or infuse information about the library; or referring friends to also participate in the SRP.

PRIZES

Most SRPs offer participants incentives for reaching various goals. Some offer one prize for the entire summer, while others create a prize structure for certain time periods, points, pages, or other specific markers. There may also be a grand prize drawing at the end of the summer for a big-ticket item such as an iPad or laptop. The planning team must decide not only how prizes will be awarded but what the prizes will be. This is often dependent upon budget, but keep in mind that many local businesses are usually willing to contribute to reading incentives. Common prizes include books or low-cost items like key chains, bracelets, and pencil cases. Offering fine waivers is a cost-free alternative and gives teens who have exceeded their fine limit the opportunity to reduce their fines and begin using the library again. Local business, both independent and chain stores, may be willing to donate gift cards or coupons for food or merchandise.

EVENTS

Depending on the size and scope of the SRP, the planning team may choose to hold events several times a week, once per summer, or anywhere in between. Many programs can be prepared once and then replicated for use in other locations. Different types of programs include:

- Book clubs
- Performers such as dancers and hypnotists
- Active classes such as martial arts or yoga
- Enrichment classes such as cooking or painting
- Crafts such as tie-dye t-shirts or jewelry making
- Contests such as paper airplanes or soap box derby

- Tournaments such as Yu-Gi-Oh! or Guitar Hero
- Games (board, card, and video)
- Movies

PARTNERSHIPS AND COLLABORATION

To engage more teens, the planning team might think about partnering with local community centers, parks and recreation departments, boys and girls clubs or other organizations which cater to youth. This could mean holding some of the library's programs at their partners' facilitators, or conducting some of the partners' programs at the library. Another way to collaborate and expand the scope of the SRP is for public libraries to work with middle and high school libraries, and vice versa. Rather than having competing programs, find ways to pool resources for a joint venture.

A KICK OFF OR FINALE PARTY

Many libraries invite SRP participants to a party at the beginning or end of the summer. If the planning team chooses to include this as part of the summer, they will need to budget for food at the minimum; entertainment and door prizes or gift bags are also often included in such events.

Budget and Fundraising

Being realistic about budget is key. The team must prioritize the components above into tiers, or categories like "must have," "preferred," and "dream." For example, the planning team may decide on the following priority areas:

- Must-have: Marketing materials and buying reading logs
- Preferred: Holding a kick-off party
- Dream: Twice-weekly programs

Each community is different so the components under each team's list of must-haves will also be different. The goal is to list only the essentials in the top tier, and keep the budget in mind when deciding what is essential.

The items in the "must have" category should be paid for by the money the library has been guaranteed, usually by its own line item in the library's operating budget or as a designated amount from the programming line item. If any money is leftover, the team should assign funds to items in the "preferred" category. On the other hand, if there is not enough money in the base budget to meet all of the "must-have" requirements, the team must either rethink their approach or begin the task of fundraising.

Most people associate fundraising with cold calling, but that is just one way to contact potential donors. First, the team must identify grants for which the library might qualify. The SRP coordinator should mark the deadline dates on a calendar and assign people to make sure the applications are submitted. With that piece taken care of, the team can concentrate on local fundraising. Before starting, read YALSA's fundraising guide, which offers advice on asking for donations, as well as templates and other fundraising tools. Find the guide at www.ala.org/givetoyalsa.

The team should also prepare by creating the following documents before approaching local businesses and organizations.

Cover Letter

Many sample letters can be found online. When searching for one to adapt to the program's needs, the team should not limit the search to library-related donation letters. Many websites feature generic letters or those created for other nonprofit community events that can be easily adapted. Include: general details about the program; local statistics such as high school reading levels or drop-out rates; statements showing how contributing to the program will help the entire community, not just the library; the date that a specific person will be following up with a phone call or in-person visit; and a brief mention of how donations will be spent, with details in the following two documents.

Sponsorship Levels

The best kind of donation is monetary, as cash can be spent how the planning team sees fit. A sponsorship differs from a donation in that in exchange for a sum of money, the donating organization's logo will appear in the SRP's marketing materials. When creating this document, the team should include levels of sponsorship, as well as places that the organization's logo will appear. An example of this can be found in Figure 1.2; each team will adapt theirs to be consistent to the size and scope of their program. In addition to a funding matrix, this document should include a list of general items or events toward which the money will go.

Platinum Sponsor $5000 +	Your logo in all print and online marketing, TV & radio commercials, and your organization mentioned at all teen SRP events
Gold Sponsor $1000-$4999	Your logo in all print and online marketing, and your organization mentioned at all teen SRP events
Silver Sponsor $500-$999	Your logo in all print and online marketing

FIGURE 1.2. Sponsorship Levels

Wish List

Requests for more individual items should be included in a wish list. It could be as specific as a wedding registry or simply a list of general items such as gift cards, books, and food. There are pros and cons to both. Naming specific items often results in getting exactly what was requested. However, there may be items that the planning team didn't even think to ask for that are more likely to be offered from an organization if the requests are more general in nature. Regardless of the specificity of the wish list, the planning team should absolutely invite ideas for donations by the organizations they contact.

Fundraising is not easy, and the library can be competing against other nonprofits in the area. Creativity helps. When following the letter up with an in-person visit, a team member might bring along a teen who will participate in the SRP. They could also bring photos of the previous summer's events or a testimonial from a teen.

No matter the amount of donations, or the size of the team's budget, the SRP will be successful if the planning team prioritizes. If the budget does not allow for all of the must-have components, the team might consider shortening the length of the program (for example, from eight weeks to six weeks). Conversely, if providing a program for the majority of the summer is top priority, the team may be forced to reduce the number of events or prizes. If the team keeps in mind the ultimate goals and objectives that were identified at the outset, the priorities will naturally follow.

Timeline

The most successful of summer reading programs are those that are well planned. Having a road map from the start of the planning process will make the preparations go more smoothly and help to decrease the panic that comes with trying to get too much accomplished as summer rapidly approaches. First, decide when the session will be and move backward. Factor in all of the components upon which the team decided during the previous stage of the planning process. Figure 1.3 is an example of a planning schedule for a program that begins in June.

Month	Task
September	Cull last year's evaluations for pertinent information to factor into decisions
	Decide upon: length of program and its dates, theme, and program components
	Sketch out a rough guide of how the base budget (before donations or grants) will be spent and what areas take priority in terms of spending
	If necessary, break into subcommittees
	Create strategy for fundraising outside of the budget allotted by administration, marking any grant deadlines on the calendar
October	Set up online work space for planning team
	Work on grant applications
	Create fundraising letter, including different levels of sponsorship, and send to local organizations
	Create tentative calendar of events
November	If any special performers or workshop facilitators will be hired, book them now
	Follow up fundraising letters with in-person visits or phone calls

FIGURE 1.3. Sample Schedule

December	Reserve rooms and spaces where programs will be held, including different branches, outside spaces, or non-library locations
	Fill in calendar of events with specific programs, confirming dates and times with performers or workshop facilitators
	Send out contracts and necessary paperwork for anyone who will be hired for a program
January	Solidify contracts
	Incorporate any grants or donations into existing budget to see if any additional SRP components can be added
	Decide upon and order incentives; determine award structure
	Decide upon registration and tracking procedures
February	Create or purchase necessary items for program, such as: reading logs, registration forms and software, promotional t-shirts, bookmarks, banners, posters, and so on
	Create library-specific marketing tools, both in print and online, such as: calendar of events, brochures and website, related booklists, and so on
March	Schedule public relations and outreach for May, including press releases to local papers & websites, appearances on local news and radio stations, and outreach to local schools or homeschool groups
	Assign a person or team to begin social media updates, increasing in frequency each month
	Decide how statistics will be kept, considering such factors as participants, program attendance, circulation, volunteerism, book reviews and more

FIGURE 1.3. Sample Schedule

April	Purchase supplies for any craft or do-it-yourself programs
	Prepare for school presentations and any other outreach appearances
	Create fact sheet for staff, so they can easily answer questions about program. Distribute fact sheets to the reference desk, checkout , and any other high traffic areas.
	Recruit volunteers
	Purchase additional copies of books on school summer reading lists
	Plan ways to incorporate the theme when decorating the building for the summer, sending a wish list of decorative items to staff, volunteers, and Friends groups
May	Create instructions for any craft or DIY programs, including samples of finished products
	Train staff and volunteers
	Make appearances in the community as planned in March
	If SRP spans more than one location, divide supplies and send to each branch
June	Begin program, including updates via social media, the library's website, and local news outlets throughout the program duration

FIGURE 1.3. Sample Schedule

With a detailed road map, a clear destination, and a dedicated team of drivers, the journey to SRP can be stress-free and rewarding.

RESOURCES

Kentucky Department for Libraries and Archives, "Planning and Organizing Your Summer Reading Program," http://kdla.ky.gov/librarians/programs/summerreading/Pages/Planning.aspx (accessed April 20, 2012)

Costley, Enid, for the Library of Virginia, "Summer Reading Program Tips for Libraries," http://libraries.idaho.gov/files/Ohio%20SR%20 Planning.pdf (accessed April 20, 2012)

FundraisingIP.com, "Writing Fundraising Letters," http://www.fund raisingip.com/fundraising/category/writing-fundraising-letters/ (accessed April 20, 2012)

Landgraf, Greg. "Summer Reading Levels Up: How Two Library Summer Reading Programs Evolved into Summer Games," *American Libraries*, Nov. 3, 2011, http://americanlibrariesmagazine.org/ features/ 11032011/summer-reading-levels (accessed April 20, 2012)

Collaboration and Partnership

Megan Honig

THE LIBRARY IS not the only institution in the community with an investment in engaging young people over the summer. Schools, community organizations, local businesses, and other municipal and regional entities all have a stake in helping teens build literacy skills and stay stimulated in the summer months. With resources tight all around, libraries now more than ever need to tap into the resources of the organizations and stakeholders around them to create successful summer reading programs (SRPs).

Collaboration can happen at a variety of levels. At the most basic level, a partner organization provides resources for the library, or the library provides resources for a partner organization, but the planning and delivery of services happens separately. For example, a local restaurant or grocery store might donate food for a summer reading celebration, or a comics or video game shop might donate merchandise for prizes. In turn, the library acknowledges the partner organization on summer reading fliers or signage. Alternatively, the library can serve as host for a program designed and led by another organization—a youth choir in need of a performance space, for instance—exposing a new network of teens to the library without expending much additional staff time.

15

At a higher level of collaboration, partner organizations work with the library to plan and deliver services together. Louisiana's East Baton Rouge Parish Library has a robust year-round partnership with the parish's juvenile detention center that includes the library bringing performers to the juvenile detention center during the summer reading program.[1] The Oakland Public Library has collaborated with local youth arts organizations Youth Speaks and BUMP Records to host an end of summer Teen Slam Jam.[2] Virtually any organization is a potential partner, including schools, recreation centers, nonprofit organizations, theaters, sports teams, homeless youth centers, cultural centers, museums, small businesses, and many more.

Why Collaborate?

There are many benefits to collaborating with outside organizations. Collaboration brings more exposure to the services the library offers. Simply by approaching potential partners, you are spreading the word about the library's mission and current offerings. Work together successfully and your partner organization will become intimately familiar with the effectiveness and commitment of your library. With the permission of schools, community centers, and other facilities frequented by teenagers, you can visit a new group of teenagers and do outreach to teens you rarely see in the library building. Take advantage of the networks that other youth-serving organizations have. Even if a local museum is unable to do programming at your library, your contact person there can still advertise the library's services on the museum's Facebook page or through other forms of outreach.

Collaborations also bring the library more resources. Quite literally in some cases: when a local business donates food or merchandise to the summer reading program, the library can save money by not having to buy food or prizes. The library may also be able to take advantage of other resources offered by partner organizations. Perhaps the documentary arts organization has a stable of laptops with fancy photo-editing software. Materials for the Arts, a program of the New York City Department of Cultural Affairs, is dedicated specifically to providing arts resources for libraries and other nonprofit institutions; find an organization in your area with a similar mission and partner with that organization to acquire materials for art and craft programs. The fresh perspective that an outsider brings is also a valuable boon for your library; a partner organization with a different mission than the library's may notice opportunities for service that the library has missed.

Getting Partnerships Started

The first step to forming effective partnerships with other organizations is to be a presence in the community. Representatives from the library should be involved in community activities, from physical events such as community board or town hall meetings to virtual participation on social networking sites and community blogs. Use the library's presence not only to comment on issues of importance to the library but also to network informally with other government agencies, schools, and organizations serving youth. Active participation will put the library in position not only to approach other organizations but to be approached. Too often, librarians assume that the community is already aware of the range of services that libraries provide, but the truth is that parents, community members, and other agencies will not always realize that libraries provide programs, meeting spaces, library orientations, and other services unless the library tells them.

The next step is to consider the library's goals. What area of the library's services should be enhanced? A mission statement, the library's or the teen department's, will help guide you here. Is the library looking to expand program offerings? Reach out to underserved populations, such as lesbian, gay, bisexual, transgender, or questioning (LGBTQ) teens, teen parents, or homeless youth? Stretch a tight budget? Support a particular kind of learning, such as science, technology, engineering, and math (STEM)? The answers to these questions will inform the kinds of partnerships the library will seek.

When library staff know the kind of collaborations that they are looking for, identify potential partners for the library. If the library is already active in the community, its staff is probably aware of many local agencies and organizations. A walk or drive around the library's neighborhood can uncover even more, as can a web search. If the library seeks a programming partner with a particular focus—say, poetry—a web search for "teens," "poetry," and the library's location can uncover a goldmine of resources.

Create a list of organizations that the library would like to partner with and reach out. Formulate a pitch that will target these specific partners. Let them know what the library envisions and what the potential benefit to the partner organization will be. Will the library make sure that all of the homeless shelter's residents get library cards? Provide a new audience for the science museum's workshop on electricity? Acknowledge the generous donation of the local bakery on the summer reading flyer? Be prepared to tell potential partners exactly why working with the library is such a great opportunity. And be open to hearing about the partner organization's vision for the collaboration, which may uncover entirely new possibilities.

Collaborating with Schools

In many ways, schools and public libraries are ideal partners for summer reading programs. Summer reading programs are designed to pick up where schools leave off, providing informal learning opportunities for students on summer vacation. Working directly with schools helps students make the transition from school to summer reading more smoothly.

Work with schools to raise awareness of the library's summer reading program among teachers and students. Meet with teachers, school librarians, and school administration to let them know what services the library offers during the summer, why summer reading is important, and how students can get involved. Schedule class visits to speak directly to students. At The New York Public Library, librarians from neighborhood branches visit middle and high schools in May and June to sign students up for the library's summer reading club. Teachers also have the opportunity to bring groups of students directly to the library for an orientation and summer reading program sign-up, which helps students become familiar with the library before the school year ends.

Of course, some schools are open during the summer, and librarians who want strong summer reading programs should include summer school students in their plans and outreach. Visit summer schools to let students know about the fun programs that the library offers during the summer months, as well as the variety of books and media available for checkout. If possible, time weekday programs so that summer school students can attend. Make sure to reach out to summer school staff early in the summer so that there is time to squeeze the library into the school's busy schedule.

Public libraries and schools should also work together to coordinate summer reading lists. Sometimes educators frustrate students and librarians, assigning out-of-print titles that are difficult for students to access or not taking advantage of the breadth of high-quality literature that is now available for teen readers. Work with teachers to suggest a diverse range of titles that will engage their students and to make sure the titles that end up on summer reading lists are ones the library can provide. Ask teachers to share their lists in advance so the library can be sure to have assigned reading on hand. Then follow up by ordering multiple copies of assigned titles well in advance of summer.

This Is Just the Beginning. . .

There is a vast array of opportunities for collaborations and partnerships that can bring the library much-needed funds, giveaways, talent, and new ideas. Collaborating with schools and other youth-serving agencies to provide an exemplary summer reading program is just one of the many ways libraries can enjoy effective partnerships. Use the relationships that the library builds during the summer reading season as a launch pad for year-round programming. Invite partner organizations to work together on even bigger projects when summer reading planning time rolls around again. Building a robust, appealing, wide-reaching young adult summer reading program can take some work, but libraries do not have to do that work alone. Reach out, and find that two heads—or two institutions each with a vision for excellent teen services—are better than one.

REFERENCES

1. Barbara Roos. "Beyond the Bars: Serving Teens in Lockdown." *Young Adult Library Services 10* (2012).
2. Oakland Public Library. "Teen Slam Jam will Rock the Oakland Public Library, Courtesy of Youth Speaks and BUMP Records," www.oaklandlibrary.org/PR/pr072308slamjam.htm (accessed Dec. 19, 2011).

Marketing, Promotion, and Outreach

Erin Downey Howerton

AS LIBRARY PATRONS age out of more traditional summer reading programs for elementary schoolers, teen services staff will face challenges to serve them effectively. Tweens and teens are a busy bunch: they may be participating in team sports, traveling with family or friends, working at the mall, or babysitting for local families. Catching their attention and offering summer reading participation options that fit their busy lifestyles can be difficult, but it can be done. The important thing is to capture a sense of novelty, especially if the library has relied on more traditional methods of promotion in the past. Fresh, new methods of raising awareness and reaching out to youth with diverse interests will help support the image of the library as a space for everyone, not just the average bookworm.

PREPARE THE BASICS

The library may base its summer reading program on a locally selected tween or teen summer reading theme or one supplied by a vendor or a collective such as the Collaborative Summer Library Program (www.cslpreads.org). No matter the theme, make sure to be consistent in use of elements like names, fonts, and graphics. Take advantage of any pre-designed templates or graphics that may be at the library's disposal—anything that is already ready for use can be a huge timesaver, especially for the staff members who wear multiple hats in the library.

Using consistent artwork will help patrons distinguish between programs by age, which is important. Make it clear to patrons who is allowed to participate in which program, as well. Because of limited funds or developmentally designated programming, many libraries choose to restrict their programs by chronological age or rising grade in school (e.g., a fifth-grader from the previous academic year is a rising sixth grader and eligible for the tween or teen program). The age issue can be very important for youth participants and their parents, so make it clear and consistent for all participants.

As previously noted, tweens and teens are busy people. They are also being marketed to in increasingly sophisticated ways. Try to make promotions as professional-looking as possible. Avoid graphics that tweens and teens may find babyish or immature, like cartoon animals or fonts like Comic Sans. Test-drive marketing materials if possible with the Teen Advisory Board or with a group of frequent customers, so to speak, so that they can help teen services staff fine-tune the SRP campaign to local tastes and preferences. Use bold, bright colors that can be identified at a distance. Keep any graphics simple so they can be scaled up or down. If time allows, ask teens themselves to help design the theme and graphics. Their pride of ownership can be a huge help in promoting the program!

Also, consider ditching the old, easily lost or misplaced paper reading and participation logs for online logs. Consider creating one that is mobile-friendly or try using existing online reading applications like LibraryThing, Goodreads, or Shelfari. Many libraries have successfully used these online resources to help facilitate online summer reading through existing group functions, and other strategies. Set up a group for your summer reading program, and tell participants to locate and join the group to "enroll." Participation in the form of writing book reviews, and having conversations online about books read is then very easy to track—and it is especially appealing to those teens who are traveling or too busy with other activities to attend in-person activities at the library. Additionally, online systems have a particular advantage over those that are (or not) turned in at the end of the summer: you can track and count partial progress towards goals, which is often substantial.

Go Where the Teens Are

Once the basic elements are in place, it's time to get out in the community. If the library markets the summer reading program only within the library itself, there is no way to target non-users or occasional users. Raising awareness in the community that the library offers summer programming for teens means increasing the library's street cred: parents will take note and tell their kids, teachers may take a flyer into their classrooms, and employers have the opportunity to offer incentives to their teen employees for participating. Remember that while the target market is teens, library staff may have to indirectly market to them through the adults in their lives, so be open to different possibilities.

Beyond schools, consider reaching out to many local organizations that cater to this age group. Good places to consider marketing the summer reading program to teens and tweens may include:

- Coffee shops or popular restaurants
- Specialty stores like skateboard or bike shops
- Recreation centers and dance studios
- Churches and religious organizations with youth-focused ministry
- Bus systems or other transportation agencies
- Local publications like school newspapers and yearbooks
- Popular attractions like swimming pools, zoos, and skate parks
- Convenience stores and gas stations
- Game stores or comic shops

Ask these organizations if they could assist in promoting the program through reduced advertising rates or a creative sponsorship—try to think of something out of the ordinary. For example, instead of posting a flyer in the local teen-friendly coffee shop, ask them if they would consider creating a special summer reading-themed drink, with a day's proceeds of sales going towards the support of the program. Perhaps the local bike or skateboard shop would sponsor a charity ride, and the teen advisory board could collect pledges and ride to raise money to fund prizes and promotional items.

Remember that the library can promote its program while increasing its resources – by providing local donors with participation recognition at the beginning of the summer, the library can promote the program out in the community. One good way to do this is through support placards. When library staff are circulating in the community and asking local business owners to support summer reading through donations of cash, in-kind services, coupons, or other incentive-type items, supply those generous donors with a placard that they can display in their storefront windows or another prominent place, such as beside the cash registers.. Designed properly, it will give the participating organization credit for supporting the summer reading program but also lead potential participants to the program through the library's website. Create generous placards, preferably tabloid sized (11″ x 17″) to accommodate large type fonts for visibility at a distance. Make a template that includes your summer reading logo, the year and date, wording that recognizes donors ("**BUSINESS NAME** is generously supporting **NAME OF TEEN READING PROGRAM**") and consider customizing each one with the name of the participating organization. Be sure to include the URL of the website, specifically leading to summer reading information. Laminating the placards will make them more durable and professional-looking. Plan to solicit donations and create the placards in time to distribute them slightly before or at the beginning of your summer reading program. This way, they will definitely double as donor recognition and as advertising. Hand-deliver the placards to participating businesses and make sure the staff member handling distribution brings tape, non-damaging adhesive, or similar products with them. Suggest the staff person volunteers to help the place the placard—then watch awareness of the summer reading program rise!

Diversify and Measure Effectiveness

While paper flyers and bookmarks have traditionally dominated summer reading promotional materials, consider using the tween and teen summer reading programs to transition away from these resource-heavy methods. By encouraging users to access information about the program and to sign up online, the library will also gain important information about where participants heard about the program. The best way to do this electronically is through the use of several distinct URLs for a singular summer reading portal online. Create unique URL redirects for a single page, and track the page hits for each individual "campaign:"

Campaign examples:

- Advertisement in Parks and Rec brochure
- Donor placard in local skateboarding shop
- Classroom television advertisement in middle school
- Flyer hung in community center
- Radio ad on station XYZ

Another way to connect mobile users to summer reading information is through the use of QR codes, or Quick Response codes. These crossword-like codes can be used by mobile phone users, who can download an app that will use the camera on the phone to decode the link and automatically open a website without the user having to type in a URL by hand. The characteristics of a good QR code are:

Mobile: the code should take the user to a mobile-optimized page on the library's website. There's nothing worse than scanning a code and being taken to a regular web page that would look fine on a 17″ monitor, but looks like Sanskrit on a phone screen.

Actionable: the code should take users to a page where they can take some sort of action, such as sign up for the program, get email reminders, or otherwise input information that allows the library to continue further interactions with them. Users should get something out of their scan.

Seamless: the information presented should tie in with every other use of the summer reading or library "brand" so that users know instantly that they scanned the correct code and are on the correct site to get the information they want.

Use a link shortener like http://bitly.com to generate a QR code for the summer reading web page, or use another QR code generator like http://qrcode.kaywa.com. It's easy to do and can help reach more tech-savvy potential summer reading participants.

Amp It Up! Fresh Spins on Old Traditions

If local teens are bored with same-old same-old methods of promotion, try some of these.

OLD METHOD: Buy shirts for your teen advisory board or teen volunteers.

AMP IT UP: Sponsor a local baseball or softball team and let them wear the library's name and logo! Grab the attention of a sports-oriented community and get the word out all summer long.

OLD METHOD: Hang fliers in local stores.

AMP IT UP: Ask a local business if the library could "borrow" their store windows for an afternoon. Rotate teen volunteers in and out as living models, posing with the merchandise and "reading" for an hour apiece. (This may work more effectively with a local retailer rather than a national chain, who may have limitations on the sorts of promotions they are allowed to do locally.)

OLD METHOD: Give away books as prizes at the end of the summer to participants who have completed their goals.

AMP IT UP: Don't wait—give away books at the beginning of the summer to those who are willing to register and set a goal. Send them off right away with a great book to get them started!

OLD METHOD: Give away bookmarks or flyers during school visits.

AMP IT UP: Work with a local high school's media production class to shoot a short (45–60 second) summer reading commercial video to be shown on local cable channels or on the school's own PA system. A coordinated radio commercial would also work great for local pop stations! Teen stars will generate interest that bookmarks can't match.

Outreach through Programming

Consider the impact of conducting summer reading programming outside the library walls. While hosting local artists, musicians, or photographers in the library is a great way to build community connections, it's also advisable to demonstrate to teens and tweens that library resources can inspire activities wherever they may be.

For example, library staff might look into bringing a crate of books on extreme sports, deck art, and biographies of famous skateboarders to the local skate shop, where they can work with the staff there to offer a program. Beach reads, romance titles, and biographies of popular celebrities might go over well at the local pool, where teen services staff could hold a program designing water-friendly jewelry or accessories like duct tape sunscreen totes. Books on cooking aimed at tweens and teens could complement a program on decorating cookies or little cakes produced by a local bakery.

Although it may be difficult to carve out time to get off the desk and out into the community, even one or two external programs can help tweens and teens make connections between library resources, the summer reading program, and their own interests. Using creativity, the knowledge that staff have of their own community, and the construction of solid local connections and partnerships, the library may extend its reach and influence.

Readers' Advisory

Maria Kramer

WITHOUT A DOUBT, summer reading is an important factor in the academic success of young people. Studies have found that participation in summer reading programs helps to prevent summer knowledge loss—a large factor in the academic gap between middle-class and low-income students. Reading is not only an entertainment option or a way of acquiring knowledge, it is a skill, and like all skills, it improves with practice and decays if ignored. This is where librarians come in, at the front lines, to help teens and tweens find books that interest them so that they can practice reading and become better and more confident readers, while exploring a variety of subjects.

Readers' advisory is also a skill that improves with practice. Finding a good book in a genre you are unfamiliar with can be a challenge—and that's a situation many general library staff, and even many youth-focused librarians, find themselves in when performing reader's advisory for teens and tweens. This chapter will provide tools and suggestions to help hone your reader's advisory skills before the summer reading rush, making reader's advisory for young adults less stressful and more fruitful for all public services staff.

Step 1: Talking to Teens

Successful readers' advisory doesn't begin with the right book list, but with the right attitude towards teen and tween patrons. The greatest list of summer reading books for young adults will be useless if teen patrons never ask for it. While teen library staff may be comfortable relating to teens, and it may even be part of the job description, other public service staff members may not be so confident. Here are some general tips to share with public services staff:

- **Catch them in the wild**: Teens will not often walk up to the desk and ask a readers' advisory question. However, teens wandering through the shelves usually react well to librarians who offer to suggest good books to them.
- **Meet them where they are:** Display enthusiasm for a teen's expressed interests, and demonstrate that the library supports those interests, e.g., "I see you like skateboarding (because you carry your board with you *everywhere*). Have you seen our collection of *Thrasher* and *Transworld Skateboarding* magazines?"
- **Perfect the art of the two-sentence book pitch:** "You like fantasy? That's awesome! This one is about a girl who fights zombies and has a sarcastic cat sidekick. She saves a prince who's been petrified for five hundred years and they fall in love while battling the ultimate evil." (This pitch is for *Sabriel* by Garth Nix.)

These suggestions can also be implemented on the large scale in terms of summer reading promotion. Don't wait for high schools and middle schools to get in touch with the teen department at the library—start scheduling visits in February or March, being mindful of spring break or standardized testing periods. Ask teachers (or teen volunteers) what the students at each school are interested in and tailor a presentation to match those interests (try the two-sentence book pitches!).

Do not underestimate the value of simply talking with young adults. Excellent, lasting library relationships can begin when a librarian walks up to a teen and asks if they would like a book suggestion. Marketing guru Seth Godin claims that businesses are most effective when they offer at least one of three things—results, thrills, and ego-stroking. Taking the time to make teen patrons feel important—stroking their egos, basically—

gives them a positive impression of the library, and makes them more likely to come back, participate in programs, and *read*—during the summer and beyond.

Step 2: Create a Summer Reading Ready Collection

As summer reading preparations begin, consider casting a critical eye at the library's YA collection and, using the resources available, ensure it is appealing to the teens that will be part of the summer reading program. Remember that the library is competing with many other sources of entertainment, not limited to video games, social media, mobile devices, and bookstores. Having a modern, appealing collection allows the library to compete with the many options that teens and tweens can use to fill their time in the summer.

Summer reading should also incorporate, on some level, three areas of collection development: books and reading material that correspond to the library's theme, whether it's independent or the annual Collaborative Summer Reading Program theme, light materials to capture the interest of teens who want a break from schoolyear reading, and books from area schools' summer reading list, if applicable. In addition, consider the following tips.

Trendspotting for the YA Librarian

One easy way to make a collection more relevant, and to better target readers' advisory is to be aware of teen literary trends. While teen literature trends wax and wane too quickly to build an entire collection around them, keeping a finger on the pulse of pop culture can help librarians better understand their patrons' interests. Here are some resources for discovering trendy fiction categories to prepare for the requests of teen and tween patrons this summer.

Lists—Lists of popular, trendy and bestselling books are great resources for getting the big picture of the teen literature landscape. Great lists for trend hunters are the *New York Times* and Amazon best sellers lists, and, of course, YALSA's book awards and booklists.

Movies and Television—A trend popular in one medium will often be popular in others as well. Be especially alert for teen books that are being made into films, as this can cause a massive spike in popularity for an entire genre. Check Nielsen ratings and box office statistics to get a broad idea of the most popular programs and films.

Pop culture resources—Staying aware of movements in popular culture at large can help librarians keep a leg up on literary trends as well. Some good resources include Teen.com, Popwatch (http://popwatch. ew.com), BoingBoing (www.boingboing.net) and io9 (www.io9.com).

Circulation statistics—Every library's community is different. Librarians can discover the trends that most popular in their communities by finding out which books are most popular among their own teen population.

General Resources

The following resources are updated each year. As summer reading prep begins, take a look at the following resources to update your collection.

Best Fiction for Young Adults (www.ala.org/yalsa/bfya)—This list, selected by YALSA members, highlights the best fiction written for readers ages 12 to 18. Check out the Top Ten version of this list for a crash course in the best YA fiction published in the past year.. (This list was formerly known as "Best Books for Young Adults" and past lists can still be found under that denomination. www.ala.org/yalsa/booklists/bbya)

Popular Paperbacks for Young Adults (www.ala.org/yalsa/booklists/poppaper)—The books on this list are specifically selected to encourage reading for pleasure, which is what summer reading is all about. Recommendations are grouped into categories for easy browsing; these categories are a good place to start trendspotting. Like the BBYA/BFYA, this list comes with a Top Ten for quick and easy selecting.

Teens' Top Ten (www.ala.org/yalsa/teenstopten)—This is a teen choice list, where actual teens nominate and vote for their favorite titles. It offers fantastic insight into what titles and genres are most popular among teens and tweens. The Teens' Top Ten nominees are announced each year in mid-April, giving library staff a list of twenty-five recent, popular books to encourage teens to read over the summer. Teens everywhere can vote on the final Teens' Top Ten at the website in August and September each year.

The Hub (www.yalsa.ala.org/thehub)—YALSA's teen literature blog, The Hub, posts content every weekday, with book reviews, lists, interviews and trendspotting. Take a trip through the archives, or subscribe for a daily dose of YA awesomeness.

Unique Audiences

When specialized questions or teen readers needing particular attention outside the librarian's usual sphere of expertise come to the desk, don't panic! Prepare by taking a look at these resources:

"DO YOU HAVE ANY BOOKS FOR BOYS?"

Guys Read (www.guysread.com)—The brainchild of author Jon Scieszka, Guys Read provides lists of boy-friendly books in such categories as "At Least One Explosion" and "How to Build Stuff." Also on the site—downloadable Guys Read bookmarks and advice for starting your own book group for dudes.

Guys Lit Wire (http://guyslitwire.blogspot.com)—The books reviewed on this blog are very diverse, from classics to horror to poetry, but the unifying theme is that they are all of particular interest to teen boys.

"MY TEENAGER DOESN'T LIKE READING. DO YOU HAVE A BOOK FOR HER?"

Quick Picks for Reluctant Young Adult Readers (www.ala.org/yalsa/booklists/quickpicks)—This YALSA list focuses on books that are high-interest, meaty, and action-oriented with compelling characters and plots. It is designed to appeal to teens who don't like to read for any reason. This list also includes a Top Ten for easy browsing.

DO YOU HAVE ANY BOOKS WITH CHARACTERS WHO AREN'T...YOU KNOW...WHITE?"

Reading in Color (http://blackteensread2.blogspot.com)—This blog reviews books featuring minority protagonists, and books written by minority authors. Often, multicultural books will be reviewed here before catching the attention of mainstream blogs, so it's a good way to get ahead of the game.

Diversity in YA (http://www.diversityinya.com/category/blog)— Fascinating essays on the issues of diversity in teen and tween lit, as well as lists of new diverse fiction for teens and tweens each month.

Graphic Novels and Manga

Graphic novels and manga can be of particular interest to reluctant readers, especially boys. The visual nature of graphic novels makes it easier for a lower-level reader to comprehend the storyline and become engaged in the plot, making them more confident as readers and more positively disposed towards reading. Additionally, while reading books may be seen as "uncool" or "unmasculine" in some peer groups, reading comic books and manga is often not.

There are a wide variety of graphic novels for all age levels and interests —including nonfiction as well as adaptations of classics, popular novels, and even TV series. The following resources can help library staff become familiar with graphic novels and manga, and build knowledge as well as the collection.

GENERAL GRAPHIC NOVEL RESOURCES

Great Graphic Novels for Teens (www.ala.org/yalsa/ggnt)—YALSA's list of the best graphic novels, fiction and nonfiction, for youth ages 12-18. If pressed for time, begin with the Top Ten list.

No Flying, No Tights (http://noflyingnotights.com/)—This site reviews primarily non-superhero comics of all types. Includes lists divided by age and genre for convenient browsing.

Core Lists from Graphic Novel Reporter (http://graphicnovelreporter.com/content/core-list-fall-2011-other)—*Graphic Novel Reporter* publishes core lists in the spring and fall of graphic novels and manga to be aware of in all age groups.

SUPERHERO COMICS

Comic Book Resources (www.comicbookresources.com)—This site is like a Voltron of blogs, a super-blog assembled from several different blogs. Absolute beginners should start with Comics Should Be Good (http://goodcomics.

comicbookresources.com), which includes plenty of "Best _____ Story Ever" lists to get new readers started in the wide world of superhero comics.

MANGA

About.com's 50 Essential Manga for Libraries (http://manga.about.com/ od/recommendedreading/tp/50-Best-Manga-For-Libraries.htm)—An excellent place to start, especially for the manga novice.

MangaBlog (www.mangablog.net)—Abundant reviews, plus links to many other manga blogs.

My Anime List (http://myanimelist.net)—Search for a title in "Manga," then click on the "Recommendations" tab. A list of user-generated read-alikes for that title will magically appear!

Step 3: Becoming a Readers' Advisory Superstar Before June 1

Think of readers' advisory in the same manner that high school students regard the SATs: studying consistently achieves better results than cramming at the last minute. There are plenty of tools and resources for YA library staff to use to build a basic RA training regimen:.

Book review blogs: If library staff are particularly weak in a specific area— for example, readers' advisory for boys, manga, multicultural literature, urban fiction—seek out blogs that address that specific topic. For blog suggestions, see Step 2.

Email discussion lists: Sign up for yalsa-bk or other library email discussion lists. Take note of RA-themed questions, and make use of recommendation compilations. Most lists have searchable archives, so if those looking for specific types of books or read-alikes for popular titles can find past recommendations.

Your own reading: Librarians and library workers typically are avid readers. Start to think of books in terms of relevant trend categories. Is it a dystopia? A paranormal romance? Try to think of three books that would appeal to someone who liked the book in question. This helps to build a personal read-alike database. Websites like Goodreads, LibraryThing and Shelfari are good for keeping track of books in this way.

Step 4: Getting Your Library on Board

Whether your library has a dedicated young adult services librarian or not, readers' advisory for teens and tweens isn't a one-person job. Nearly every person who works with teens or tweens at the public library—which is everyone who works at the public library—will have the opportunity to answer a young adult reader's advisory question. Teen and tween library staff can help support non-YA staff in this endeavor before summer reading begins by taking the following actions.

- Create read-alike lists and pathfinders for popular trends and titles. Depending on the library's infrastructure, these can be stored physically, on a staff intranet, or on the library's public website.
- Write a regular book review series for the library's blog or Facebook page to help generate awareness of teen and tween books for staff and the public.
- Present on teen readers' advisory at a staff training or a summer reading planning meeting, sharing tools from this chapter.

When an entire library is united in the goal of encouraging reading for teens and tweens, truly remarkable things can be achieved.

Summer reading is a time to encourage teens to read for pleasure and personal interest—not because they are required to do so. By introducing youth to books, libraries help them succeed academically, explore new worlds and new points of view, learn more about themselves and others, and, most importantly, have fun. Readers' advisory also is a gateway into creating relationships with teens and promoting a positive image for the library. There's nothing quite like the magical moment when a librarian matches a teen with that perfect book. The approaches in this chapter should lead to many of those moments.

Technology

Chris Shoemaker

LIBRARIES SERVE AS destinations for more than just traditional print materials, offering an array of digital services as well as informal learning opportunities through programs. While many libraries post their reading lists online and handle registration through an online database, there are additional strategies for virtual library engagement during summer reading. The summer reading program is an excellent opportunity for libraries to expand their online programs and services, and increasing their digital portfolio is an essential step for libraries to continue to engage teens throughout the summer in an online world.

According to a 2011 Pew Internet and American Life study on online behaviors in users under 30, 53 percent report spending time online to pass time, with no specific uses in mind.[1] Eighty percent of teens use social networking sites, with Facebook topping out at 93 percent of online teens. Older teens use their time online to interact with friends and create content, while younger teens spend their online time playing games.[2]

Libraries can encourage additional teen involvement simply by incorporating those online behaviors into existing summer reading programs. In a 2009 article in *School Library Journal*, YA librarian Jessica Wooten discusses her success in "joining reading with an opportunity for creative expression."[3] Melding together reading and creative opportunities also addresses a common developmental need of teens, specifically a constructive use of time, an idea that is already at the heart of summer reading programs.[4] While it can be tempting to look to the traditional school year for examples of structure, it is important to build a summer reading program that differs from the academic experience and incorporating digital elements addresses that need. The Wallace Foundation, in a 2009 paper by Terzian, Moore, and Hamilton, addressed the need for summer learning programs to be different from academia through interactive and cultural enrichment activities.[5] Moving book reviews and discussions to a social platform, introducing virtual and physical badges as incentives, remixing audio-visual content—these are activities that students do not traditionally engage in during formal classroom learning times, but are opportunities for self-guided learning experiences.

Without the schedule of traditional classes in summer, teens have the opportunity to engage in more informal learning opportunities at a variety of different engagement levels. Mimi Ito and her collaborators in "Hanging Out, Messing Around, Geeking Out" discuss various levels of engagement: low level hanging out, mid-level messing around, and high-level geeking out.[6] Summer programming easily fits into this model, from one-off events to to monthly themed projects to summer long discussion sessions. A standalone video game program provides opportunities for teens who are only able to drop into programs, while a multisession video editing project encourages greater participation and can cover higher level material. A multi-month game design program allows topics to be examined in depth, provides opportunities for teens to display their talents and interests, and keeps them connected with the library throughout the summer. This formula can easily be remixed to support a wide array of teen interests and projects that can be realized at any library.

While providing access to technology services can be complicated, libraries are already destinations for teens looking to use computers and connect to free wifi. Reserving a computer to serve as a dedicated summer reading terminal allows teens to explore the websites used in the program without forcing them to choose between a library program and recreational Internet use. Teens with smartphones or wifi-equipped MP3 players have access to a wide range of apps and mobile versions of websites, and gaming platforms such as SCVNGR incorporate text messaging into play, providing access to standard cell phone users as well. Funding for summer reading programs differs wildly, and bringing in technology to programs and services can mean increased cost, whether it's through staff time, hardware, or software. However, many resources that are free for use can easily be incorporated into summer reading programs, and libraries may be able to enter into mutually beneficial partnerships with service providers to advance the goals of the library and the goals of the service provider. Websites such as Goodreads, LibraryThing, Delicious, and Pinterest are all available for free. SCVNGR, a location-based social gaming platform, provides registered users with a small number of free credits, and then charges a fee for more complex services.

In 2010, The New York Public Library, Queens Library, and Brooklyn Public Library relaunched their collaborative summer reading program (SRP), bringing in social elements, gaming, and content creation. The revised SRP website allows users to create their own user names and customized avatars, while encouraging them to post reviews and promote the reviews of their friends. Participants earn badges for visiting their library, for participating in programs, for contributing reviews, and more. Library staff are able to create custom badges and award them for special programs, top reading accomplishments, or other activities. Users are also able to track their summer reading participation online, but they are also able to print out certificates their avatars, their reading lists, and their badges earned. By incorporating technology into their summer reading program, New York City librarians are able to engage with youth in a variety of ways.

Funding is a major consideration when developing technology platforms, and it may not be possible to build a custom website. However, libraries can look towards a variety of solutions to bring digital resources into their programming.

FREE TECHNOLOGY TOOLS

Goodreads

With nearly 7 million users and a catalog of 230 million books, Goodreads has become a popular site for readers to track their reading and to get reading recommendations. Registered users are able to build reading lists, mark books as read, rate books, and write reviews. When used as part of the summer reading program, Goodreads enables teens to record their reading habits and share reviews with their friends. Providing a virtual forum for participation can encourage teens who are shy or uncomfortable speaking in a traditional discussion group to contribute their ideas. It also allows users to engage in the summer reading process when they travel or are unable to make it into the library for sharing opportunities. Goodreads can also be installed as an app on a Facebook page, allowing teens and libraries to share their reading in a greater social sphere. Libraries can promote their summer lists, highlight reviews, and encourage readers to discuss the titles online.

Cost and consideration: While the site is free to use, there are ads included on the book pages. As Goodreads is a public social site, librarians may have concerns for online privacy and safety, but this provides a good opportunity to discuss online identity. Teens must be at least 13 to use the site.

Pinterest

One of *Time*'s top 50 sites of 2011, Pinterest is a social service in which users are able to build custom vision boards by compiling images and videos from other users and from websites.[7] Registered users are able to remix content, share it with their followers, and comment on the material. Libraries looking to build additional engagement with their summer reading programming can have participants build boards that explore the theme through multimedia content. Those boards can be displayed in online albums or on library display spaces, and weekly favorites can be selected throughout the course of the summer reading program. Allowing users to create their own summer reading visual experience may increase participant buy-in and build trans-media literacy skills. Building a board of bats and nocturnal creatures, a board of movies and television shows about sleep, and a board of sunset photos explores a nighttime theme and involves multiple interpretations.

Cost and consideration: Pinterest requires interested users who must be at least 13 to request an invitation to the service. Accounts can be linked to Facebook or Twitter, allowing for multiple streams of content posting and commenting.

SCVNGR

A location-based social gaming platform, SCVNGR encourages players to record their visits via text message or the SCVNGR app. Players can also engage in challenges at the site, such as taking and uploading photos, answering questions, or scanning QR codes. While not all types of phones will be able to handle all challenges, the broad nature of the challenges provide plenty of opportunity for participation. Library can create a SCVNGR trek that incorporates popular community destinations, summer reading partners, or multiple library branches. Treks could also be created around summer reading themes—a food theme could involve a stop at a farmers' market, a visit to the library's cookbook collection and then an outdoor cooking demonstration sponsored by the library, with challenges at each stop. SCVNGR also awards participants badges, which helps track progress through the trek. Libraries can use existing gaming platforms without having to custom build their own, incorporating educational resources into an informal learning process.

Cost and consideration: Basic service is free, allowing users five credits to create their trek. Additional credits are available for a price. SCVNGR is available as an app for Apple and Android, but not for BlackBerry. There are limited play-through options with text messaging. Users with devices that lack a GPS will have a more difficult time participating.

Stroome

YouTube might be towards the top of most-visited sites for library computers, but video programming in the summer should encompass more than passively viewing clips. There are alternatives to expensive video editing software, one of which is Stroome, a web-based video editor. Users are able to upload video clips, do simple cuts, add transitions, build soundtracks, and then publish the finished projects to the site. In addition to uploading and editing their own film, members are able to work collaboratively on projects. A team of teen videographers could explore their neighborhood, looking for counter-culture shops and art venues, record interviews with members of the community, and collaboratively edit the final project for an underground themed program. They could also create promotional book trailers for the summer reading lists. These interactive media projects allow participants to build their digital skill sets and enable them to easily promote the finished project across a variety of platforms. The ease of publication allows feedback from the creator's peer circle, while also highlighting the resources and services of the library.

Cost and consideration: Stroome provides their tools for free, but there is a 3 gigabyte storage limit. Library computers must have up-to-date software to run the video editor and must have the drives needed to upload videos from digital cameras. The content on Stroome can run toward the academic side, which may discourage teens from exploring the video offerings already online.

The easiest way to decide what technology to incorporate into a summer reading program is to talk to the teen participants and find out whether they are interested in socializing their book discussions, adding in game components, or developing videos. Not all aspects will appeal to every community, and it's important to have teen participants involved in the process of developing their summer reading program. Advancing summer activities, in both traditional and technological routes, serves to broaden both the audience and the awareness of the program, and strengthens the role of the library within the community.

Keeping Up with Technology Trends

Even the most tech-savvy library staff can be overwhelmed by the cutting edge and find it difficult to stay on top of trends and new developments. For the latest technology tools that cross over easily into the library world, keep an eye on the following resources.

Mashable
www.mashable.com
Dedicated to social media, technology, and digital culture, Mashable features top news stories, popular GIFs, trends in technology, and tips and tricks for staying engaged in the rapidly changing online world.

NYC Collaborative Summer Reading Program
www.summerreading.org
A tri-library initiative with the Brooklyn Public Library, Queens Library, and The New York Public Library, this is the home page for the summer reading program.

Teen Tech Week™

www.ala.org/teentechweek

This national technology program from YALSA works to educate teens on bot the ethics and the uses of technology.

YALSA Blog

http://yalsa.ala.org/blog

Find out what YALSA members around the country are doing with technology and programming, including recommended apps, popular websites, and potential ideas for advancing digital offerings at your library.

YPULSE

www.ypulse.com

While YPULSE is not focused on technology, the media research available on the site is helpful for developing program ideas, staying on top of trends, and creating marketing plans.

REFERENCES

1. Rainie, Lee. "The Internet as a Diversion and Destination," Pew Internet & American Life Project, Nov. 15, 2011, www.pewinternet.org/Reports/2011/Internet-as-diversion.aspx (accessed Dec. 15, 2011).
2. Madden, Mary. "Teens, Social Network Sites & Mobile Phones: What the Research Is Telling Us" Pew Internet & American Life, Dec. 5, 2011, www.pewinternet.org/Presentations/2011/Dec/COSN.aspx (accessed Dec. 18, 2011).
3. Wooten, Jennifer. "Flipped! Want to Get Teens Excited about Summer Reading? Just Add Video" *School Library Journal* (May 2009): 38–40.
4. Search Institute, "40 Developmental Assets for Adolescents," www.search-institute.org , www.search-institute.org/content/40-developmental-assets-adolescents-ages-12-18 (accessed Dec. 18, 2011)
5. Terzian, Mary, Kristin Anderson Moore, and Kathleen Hamilton. "Effective and Promising Summer Learning Programs and Approaches for Economically-Disadvantaged Children and Youth: A White Paper for the Wallace Foundation," Wallace Foundation, July 10, 2008, www.wallacefoundation.org/knowledge-center/summer-and-extended-learning-time/summer-learning/Documents/Effective-and-Promising-Summer-Learning-Programs.pdf (accessed Dec. 18, 2011).
6. Ito, Mizuko, et al. "Hanging Out, Messing Around, and Geeking Out: Kids Living and Learning with New Media." MIT Press, http://mitpress.mit.edu/catalog/item/default.asp?ttype=2&tid=11889 (accessed Dec. 18, 2011).
7. McCracken, Harry. "The 50 Best Websites of 2011." *Time*, Aug. 16, 2011, www.time.com/time/specials/packages/0,28757,2087815,00.html (accessed June 15, 2012).

Evaluation

Mark Flowers

Whether a summer reading program is wildly successful, disappointing, or somewhere in between, evaluation is crucial to determining what happened and why, and how to improve the program in the future. As Sarah Flowers puts it:

> Evaluation itself is not the goal; rather, the focus of evaluation should be on improvement: how to improve the services you offer, how to work smarter, how to have the best possible library programs and services that improve the lives of not only teens but your whole community.[1]

Given that the purpose of evaluation is to improve the program, there are still a number of questions that must be answered before designing an evaluation.

- Which aspects of the program will be evaluated
- The best evaluation tool to use
- How to use the evaluation data to make changes in the program
- Who needs to see the data and how to present it

These are the questions that this chapter will attempt to answer.

EVALUATION TOOLS

Before determining what evaluation tools to use, the librarian evaluating the program should know what changes she is willing or able to make to the program: there is no point in collecting data on aspects of a program that cannot or will not be changed. Regardless of what data is collected, all evaluation tools should be in place before the program is launched; having evaluation tools in place well before the program begins allows access to the most effective data.

Depending on the library, teen community, and library staff, a summer reading program may include any number of the following goals:

- Improving reading skills
- Increasing enjoyment of reading in the community
- Attracting teens into the library over the summer
- Offering fun summer activities

These goals should be articulated during the planning phase of the program, and evaluation tools should be chosen that will best measure the outcome of each goal. Some goals can be easily assessed with a single evaluation tool. Others may require multiple methods of evaluation. Discussed below are a number of common evaluation tools, but depending on how specific the goals of the program, librarians evaluating their SRPs may have to create their own evaluation tools. The most important point is to be sure that the tool measures something specific about the program's goal.

DATA COLLECTION

As C.M. Koontz points out, program evaluation can be divided into two aspects: evaluation of customer behavior and evaluation of customer satisfaction.[2] Customer behavior in a summer reading program can be relatively straightforward to collect. Many libraries have built-in requirements to report SRP statistics to the state. The reporting form may look something like Figure 6.1.

Total Teens Registered	
Total Goals Set	
Total Goals Met	
Total Programs	
Total Attendance	

FIGURE 6.1. Reporting Form

These basic numbers—when compared to previous years, to other libraries, and to other departments—can be used to evaluate such goals as increasing the number of teens involved in SRP since last year and offering enjoyable programs over the summer.

Robyn Lupa cautions against comparing a teen program with a children's program, saying that since teens "can choose to attend your program the numbers will be fewer, while children's [programs] . . . are almost always guaranteed a full house."[3] But a careful teen librarian may still be able to make useful comparisons. A librarian may know, for instance, that teen programs generally draw 10 percent of the attendance of children's programs at the library. If the library's children's department garnered five hundred registrations, the librarian can then use fifty as a rough standard to use to evaluate how effectively the library marketed the teen program and whether the program achieved its goal of bringing in a large number of teens.

Data collection should not end at counting up the number of enrollees. Numbers of participants at individual events should be collected as well. This can be done either by counting the total number of people attending, or by breaking down the numbers in a variety of ways. For example, for longer events like a gaming day staff can count attendance at half-hour or hour increments. Or at events with multiple attractions, like a crafts event, staff can count attendance by craft table. Similarly, data can be broken down by age levels, either simply teen vs. non-teen (parents, younger siblings) or more detailed: children, tweens, younger teens, older teens, adults, and so on. The import of many of these numbers should be obvious. If a particular art table garnered 40 percent of the participants and another only 10 percent or less, it should be easy to adjust the program in the future to better reflect the habits of the participants. Similarly, if 85 percent of the attendance at a gaming day took place between the hours of noon and 2 p.m., but it was staffed for six hours, this is clearly a waste of resources, and the next time it can focus on only those two popular hours. Of course the data will not always be so clear cut, and librarians may have to make tough decisions, but this basic data will allow these tough decisions to be informed decisions.

Collecting data about customer behavior can generate valuable information, but many of the goals that teen librarians set will require collecting information about customer attitudes and satisfaction. This data can be more tricky to collect.

Surveys

Rhea Joyce Rubin says surveys "are best used when you need information from the participant's perspective" and have the advantages of being relatively inexpensive, systematic, and easy to analyze.[4] Many of the satisfaction and outcome-based goals of a SRP can be assessed through well-designed surveys. Individual events can be evaluated by asking participants to fill out a short survey of three or four questions:

- Did you enjoy the event?
- How did you hear about it?
- Would you come back?
- What could be improved?

Analyzing the data from these surveys can be challenging, particularly with open-ended questions, but trends still emerge. Start by entering as much of the data as possible into a spreadsheet so that the data can be sorted in multiple ways. For example, using the above questions, a librarian evaluating an event may sort together all the survey responses that said they enjoyed the event and compare them to those who said they didn't. Then the librarian can look at the differences in each group's answers to the other questions. Presumably most or all of those who did not enjoy the event said they would not come back, but far more important is how many of those who said they did enjoy it would come back. Similarly, there may be differences in how the two groups heard about the event. Perhaps those who enjoyed it were more likely to have heard about it from a friend and had fun because they were with their friends; meanwhile those who did not enjoy the event may have been more likely to hear about it as they walked into the library and didn't feel as comfortable.

The next step is to apply these trends to the SRP's goals. If a goal was to create an enjoyable event and only 50 percent of participants said they enjoyed it, changes are clearly necessary, but what those changes will be depend on the answers to the other questions. Because the teens who did not enjoy the event may have felt uncomfortable because they were at the program alone, the program could be improved either by making the program more welcoming or by focusing marketing on creating word of mouth, rather than trying to cajole teens in on the day of the program. At the same time, an entirely different goal of the event may have been to increase skills in a craft, and it is possible that this goal may have been met even by those who said they did not enjoy it. This is why it is so important to have clear goals and evaluation tools that address those goals: the numbers alone do not make a successful or unsuccessful program.

More complex questions about SRPs as a whole can be addressed by administering before-and-after surveys. For example everyone who signs up for the SRP can be given a quick survey:

- How much do you like reading?
- How much do you read a week?
- What kinds of books do you like?
- How well do you feel you understand what you read?

The same survey can then be given to anyone who completes the program—if they can be tracked down, it can be just as valuable to get this information from teens who didn't finish the program. These surveys can be given out by hand to each participant, or the library may set up an online survey on a site like SurveyMonkey (www.surveymonkey.com). If the library collects email addresses or cell phone numbers on the registration cards, the link can be emailed or texted to all participants.

This type of tool can help evaluate goals such as improving reading enjoyment or improving reading skills. In analyzing these surveys, librarians will use some of the same techniques as the event surveys, but will be additionally comparing the before and after answers, such as whether teens said they enjoyed reading more after the program than before, or if they said that they read more hours a week. With self-evaluation questions like "How well do you feel you understand what you read?" it is important to keep in mind Rubin's warning that "asking participants about their knowledge or skill level does not really assess that; instead, surveys measure what the participant perceives to be true." This doesn't mean asking the question is pointless, just that the evaluator should be clear about what is being assessed. Additionally, this data must be handled carefully if only teens who finished the program complete the after survey—the program may have simply weeded out the teens who don't like reading. That is why it is ideal to get after surveys from non-completers. To address this last issue, staff can ask teens to include their names on the surveys or attach them to their registration cards, so the data set includes the same group before and after. If staff or teens are uncomfortable with having names attached to the surveys, each teen can mark his survey with a simple code or a number associated with the registration card.

Focus Groups

If there are enough participants in a SRP it may be possible to put together a focus group to discuss the program. Focus groups can gather more detailed and longer answers to evaluation questions. Focus groups should include six to ten teens—if possible, a mix of teens who did and did not complete the program, perhaps even one or two who did not register at all. They should last thirty to sixty minutes, and include snacks or some other incentive to make it worthwhile for the participants. The facilitator should ask open-ended questions to encourage participation. Since a thirty-minute focus group will not answer everything staff want to know about the SRP, questions should focus on specifically addressing the goals for the program. The facilitator should record the session or take copious notes, so the group's answers can be analyzed just as rigorously as answers from a survey.

As Rubin notes, focus groups are not helpful in "assess[ing] an individual's progress or achievements." Rather, they are most "useful when identifying outcomes and indicators."[5] This means that focus groups will not be useful for assessing goals such as improved reading skill or reading enjoyment. They can be very helpful, though, in assessing the overall satisfaction with the program, problems with implementation, marketing, and more. As always, questions should be based on aspects of the program which can realistically be changed.

Staff Evaluation

A teen librarian's colleagues can be an invaluable, if more informal, source of information about the program. Most teen librarians are intimately aware of their SRP and how it works, but coworkers aren't necessarily. They should be asked if the registration and prize information made sense. Was everything easy to fill out and intuitive? Did teens ask questions about the program they were unable to answer? How can the program be made easier for them to understand and implement?

Similarly, an individual teen librarian will almost certainly not talk with every participant in the SRP, but someone on the library staff may have. Staff can be probed for their impressions of the teens. Did they seem enthusiastic about the program or were they being pressured to sign up by parents or friends? Did they ask a lot of questions about prizes and events or just register and go? This level of evaluation will be much more anecdotal, but at the very least, it can help make the job of coworkers easier, which is a great goal in itself.

CONCLUSION

Regardless of the tools used, the data collected, and the analysis made, the most important step in evaluation is to actually put it to use. As already noted, some evaluation data is often required by supervisors, by the state library, or both. Other data may be needed to present a report to a Friends group that funded the program. These are relatively simple uses of the data. Most significant are those that make improvements to the program, such as those proposed previously, but there may be even further uses for evaluation data. Good data, especially over the course of multiple years, can be essential for advocating for more support or materials from supervisors or Friends groups. If the data show that participation has increased by 50 percent and satisfaction by 25 percent over the course of three years on a limited budget, a teen librarian may be able to convince the library to devote more resources to the teen program in the future. No matter the outcome of such advocacy and improvements, a great teen librarian will continue to evaluate and collect data about all of the library's teen programs. Ideally, evaluation should be an integral component in every program or service offered, such that it allows for an endless feedback loop: a program is developed, then implemented, then evaluated; the results of the evaluation are then used to retool and redevelop the program, for further implementation, and further evaluation.

REFERENCES

1. Flowers, Sarah. *Evaluating Teen Services and Programs: A YALSA Guide.* New York: Neal-Schuman, 2012.
2. Koontz, C.M." How to Assess Your Marketing Effectiveness," *Marketing Library Services* 18 (May/June 2004): 6-8.
3. Lupa, Robyn. "Programming for 'Tweens and Young Teens" *in Serving Young Teens and 'Tweens,* ed. by Sheila B. Anderson. Westport, Conn.: Libraries Unlimited, 2007.
4. Rubin, Rhea Joyce. *Demonstrating Results: Using Outcome Measurement in Your Library.* Chicago: ALA, 2006, 47.
5. Ibid.

Program Examples

EACH SUMMER, HUNDREDS of public libraries (and some school libraries) host summer reading programs, designed for two purposes: to attract teens and tweens to fun, free activities at the library and to diminish summer learning loss among teens and tweens.

Libraries conduct a variety of events, including reading-incentive programs, in which teens and tweens can win prizes by reading a specific number of pages or for a specific number of hours, or activity programs, including games, crafts, food and more. In this chapter, YALSA highlights the innovative reading incentive programs and activity programs collected from its members, as well as activity ideas to highlight the Teens' Top Ten booklist. In addition, sidebars will provide guidance on planning food programs without too much mess, volunteer programs, games, budget concerns, and more.

READING INCENTIVE PROGRAMS

Reading incentive programs still comprise a majority of tween and teen summer reading programs across the country. Over the years, library

VOLUNTEER PROGRAMS AND YOUTH PARTICIPATION

Merideth Jenson-Benjamin is a Teen Services Librarian at the Glendale (Ariz.) Public Library, and she has worked with her Teen Library Council (TLC) to have them plan and produce programs. Here is her process.

It all starts with my TLC group. I recruit 10-15 TLC kids, usually from my summer volunteers. I have anywhere from 35 to 50 teens volunteer for me each summer, so I have a pretty good group to choose from. I try to recruit kids from different schools, with varied interests, but the real key is enthusiasm. The TLC kids are the most motivated and involved kids I have.

Before the first meeting, I talk to each TLC member, and tell them that they will need to develop a goal for the year. Their goal is something that they would like the group to focus on. It can be anything, as long as it is 1) teen focused and 2) ties back to our mission. That's pretty vague, so I also give them a sheet of guidelines. I also try to get them talking to each other. Facebook is a good tool for this, but I've also used Google Groups.

At the first meeting of the year, I have the teens brainstorm with each other. I have a form that helps them to get thinking in a library way. It asks them to think about what they want to accomplish, what the costs would be, both in terms of staff and money. It also asks them for "challenges" and "opportunities" associated with the project.

Two Things About Your Goal

1. **It needs to fit in with the library mission.** You can find the library mission statement here: www.glendaleaz.com/library/Mission.cfm. You need to tie your goal back to this mission statement. It's not hard to do.

2. As you think about what you would like the Teen Library Council to accomplish this year, remember that your goal needs to be SMAART. What is SMAART? Look below!

   - **S – Specific.** Your goal needs to be something specific. "More video game tournaments" is not specific. "To Host a Just Dance Tournament for Teen Tech Week 2012" is. Be definite about what you want to achieve.

   - **M – Meaningful.** Make your goal something you actually care about. If you don't care about the Teen Facebook page, don't make your goal something to do with Facebook. Your goal needs to be something that you are going to want to invest time and effort into.

- **A – Actionable**. Don't say you're not going to do something. The lack of action is not action. So don't say: "The Teen Department will not buy any more Justin Beiber CDs." That's not something you DO. Your goal needs to be something that we can work towards, not something we should stop doing.

- **A – Achievable**. Please, for the love of Aquaman, be realistic. You may say, "The Library will build a teen annex featuring 103 inch flat screen TVs and a recording booth." However, you and I and the rest of the rational universe know that is not going to happen. So think about what we can actually achieve in the next 10 months.

- **R – Relevant**. The goal needs to be focused on Teens in the library. You are the Teen Library Council, this is what you do. So while you may feel strongly that the DVD collection needs major work, that is not a teen focused goal, and not something we can work on.

- **T – Timely.** This one's easy! You have until July 31. That's it. So think about that when you're thinking about your goal being attainable.

Often, more than one kid will have a similar idea, so this is a good chance for them to connect, if they haven't already. We encourage the kids to work in small groups or with a partner, it's a skill builder for them, and a form of insurance for us; if one kid flakes out, there are two or three to pick up the project.

After some brainstorming they present their goals. I've experimented with a few ways of doing this. In 2010, they had to compress their goal into a tweet—they only had 140 characters to get their idea across. In 2011, each teen/group had two minutes to "pitch" their idea to the group. I and my teen services co-worker listen to each pitch and ask some questions. I've never had to kill an idea outright, but sometimes they evolve in interesting ways based on budget and policy!

More often than not, the goals are program-based. However, I have had kids suggest other ideas. Last year, I had one young lady want to revamp our genre labeling system, and others want to change the review forms and set up a display area for those reviews.

Also at the first meeting, we make a rough calendar of when all these programs could happen. I've found that getting a rough date on the calendar makes the Powers That Be a little calmer about teens producing programs and also impresses on the kids that this is real and they need to be serious. It also lets everybody know where their energy should be focused.

After the first meeting, I share their ideas with my managers, to get a feel for the climate, yes, but more to show off how awesome and creative my teens are. I then communicate with each group or kid individually. I give them any notes the staff might have, and make suggestions for the next step.

For example two of my girls want to plan a "geek day" kind of a minicon. I asked them to think about what kinds of activities such a day would include, and who we could partner with in the community – local fan groups and clubs, etc.

As their ideas firm up, I give each group a programming form. This was something I adapted from someone on the YA-YAAC email list, and it's what I and the other teen staff use when we plan. It's similar to the brainstorming form, but asks for more details and specifics.

At the actual events, it is understood that the teens who planned the event will be there, and that it is their responsibility to set up, do any pre-prep, watch the clock, mediate disagreements, clean up, and all of the thousand other little things that come up in a program. There is always a staff member there to back them up. Also, one or two other TLC members who are not directly involved in the project will come to help out.

In writing this out, I realize this sounds like a lot of work, and it is! However, I know that the programming my library offers is much more in tune with my community and with what my kids want.

cooperatives have produced program themes with manuals, reading lists, graphics, reading logs, and other materials to help individual libraries plan their own programs. Some libraries still conduct their own independent programs with their own themes. This section details creative and successful reading incentive programs from libraries around the United States.

TEEN SUMMER PASSPORT PROGRAM
Oakland (Calif.) Public Library

The Oakland Public Library started its Teen Summer Passport Program in 2009, running it all summer long at all seventeen branches of the library. The program was open to anyone between 12 and 18 years old from early June to August. The program combines the reading incentive program with exploration of the cultural, educational, and recreational opportunities in the San Francisco Bay Area. The library created a list of museums, farmers' markets, cemeteries, art openings, skate parks, youth centers, parks, and specific destinations like Oakland Chinatown or Lake Merritt. The library also encouraged teens to visit a beach, see a movie, go to a baseball game, and attend a street fair with a list of locations. When teens signed up for the program, they received a passport and the list of locations and activities. They received a stamp in their passports for each site visit, as well as for writing a book review or a poem. They could earn up to eighteen stamps, and for every three stamps they received a raffle ticket (they could earn up to six); after nine stamps (three raffle tickets) they received a USB drive. Raffle prizes included six iPod shuffles, purchased with library funds, and the grand prize was a computer donated by the City of Oakland's computer provider, PC Professional. The program ended with a party at the Main Library's TeenZone with performances by hip-hop artists from the local organization, Youth Uprising, and with the drawing for the raffle prizes.

Brian Boies is one of six Teen Service Librarians who serve the seventeen branches of Oakland Public Library. He and the other librarians encouraged teens in the program to read books and write reviews to earn stamps, but they also encouraged the teens to experience the world outside traditional library walls and resources. The librarians asked their teen regulars for feedback about the Passport Program idea, and teen volunteers helped to staff the Passport stations in each branch to give teen participants their stamps and rewards.

The library used its annual teen services budget to provide $2,000 that paid for printing the passports, registration cards, staff guidelines, book review forms, and the instruction sheets with the list of suggested "Hot Spots" for teens to visit; 200 flash drives; six iPods; snacks for the

WORKING WITH TEENS WITH SPECIAL NEEDS

Libraries are open to anyone, so it is important to conduct summer reading programs that welcome any teen, no matter their abilities. While planning activities, events, or reading incentive programs, please consider ways to include teens with physical disabilities, teens who speak English as a second language, teens with learning disabilities, teens on the autism spectrum, or any other youth who find themselves outside the mainstream.

Summer Reading Incentives for Everyone

One simple way to ensure that any teen or tween can participate in the summer reading program is to broaden the definition of participation – count pages read versus number of books, allow teens to select any type of material from any section of the library, and allow teens to count minutes listened to audiobooks. Here are two good examples from the field.

At Baraboo Public Library in Wisconsin, the Great Summer Teen Read-a-Thon opened its reading incentive by allowing teens to track minutes read or minutes listening to audiobooks. This broadened participation, allowing all teens to participate, providing them a chance to find alternatives to books or to engage with material no matter their reading skill level. All teens in the community were welcome to register and participate and contribute minutes toward the 200,000 minutes goal to get gaming consoles and games into the public library.

The Washington-Centerville Public Library in Ohio saw benefits to broadening their reading rules, too. Teens could read juvenile fiction titles, in addition to YA and adult books, or could listen to audiobooks to count toward their reading entries in the Teen Summer Reading Club.

Programming Tips

- Ensure that library programs are accessible to anyone—sponsor activities that allow teens with physical disabilities to participate, bring in a sign language interpreter for presentations and speakers for teens and tweens who are deaf or have auditory disabilities, make sure that your library offers access to Braille or large-print books, and let teens who qualify know they can find books through the National Library Service for the Blind and Physically Handicapped.

- Plan read-aloud sessions, where teens can read selections from their favorite books to each other or listen to audiobook recordings. Pair a read-aloud program with the children's summer reading program.
- Many libraries offer ESL Speaking Cafés for adults, wherein English language learners can practice their skills in a relaxed setting. Libraries can offer a similar program for teens, tweens, and their parents.
- Teens and tweens on the autism spectrum can sometimes have difficulty with bright lights or loud noises. The Joint Library offers tips for programming for youth on the spectrum at www.thejointlibrary.org/autism/strategies.htm.
- When doing school visits, check in with the special education staff. Bring flyers for parents with contact information for the teen library staff to discuss how to include youth with special needs
- Use inclusive language on the library's website, summer reading program website, and in flyers—make it clear that all teens are welcome at the library.

final party; and miscellaneous supplies for each branch. The total cost came to $2,401.94 for more than 600 teens.

For the 2011 program, the library made minor changes, basically to establish direct partnerships with community groups and to promote specific art events by giving double passport credit, and to encourage teens to post book reviews on the library's new website. The library intends to continue the Passport Program every summer, and hopes to expand it once Teen Services is more fully staffed.

THE GREAT SUMMER TEEN READ-A-THON
Baraboo (Wisc.) Public Library

In the summer of 2007, the Baraboo Public Library ran the Great Summer Teen Read-a-Thon, a ten-week-long reading program for those who had completed grades six through twelve. The program asked teens to count their time spent reading; if they collectively read 200,000 minutes during the summer, the library promised to purchase video consoles and games to use during regularly scheduled gaming nights at the library. Local doctors' offices donated money to the library to purchase active games such as Wii Sports and Dance Dance Revolution to help teens gain fitness benefits from playing games at the library.

Teen specialist Penny Johnson began advertising the program in May through school visits and brochures; the library also started soliciting monetary donations in early May. Registration for the program began the Monday after the last day of school in June; the library ordered the standard reading charts offered by Upstart as part of the Collaborative Summer Library Program (CSLP) program so teens could keep track of their reading minutes, and the library kept record of the minutes in a computer database. Posters placed around the library gave a running count of the progress throughout the summer. By the end of ten weeks, teens in Baraboo read a total of 245,000 minutes, so at the end of August the library purchased a new Wii system and a used Playstation 2 system along with two DDR pads. The total cost came to $300, which was fully funded by the donations from the doctors' offices.

The library held its first gaming night with the new systems and games in mid-September, with seventy teens in attendance. Johnson said that the population of Baraboo is around 11,000 with a service area of 18,000. The middle school and high school have a combined enrollment of 1,850 students. The possibility of getting new gaming systems and games for the teens to play at the library was highly motivating, and Johnson said that she hasn't seen anything else create such excitement among Baraboo's teens. She has offered different incentives in subsequent summers, such as netbooks for use in the library and a teen music CD collection, but nothing has matched the game systems for generating enthusiasm.

Library staff and teen volunteers helped teens register for the program and helped with the recordkeeping throughout the summer. Johnson recommended *Gamers in the Library?!* by Eli Neiburger.

YOU ARE HERE

Rebecca M. Arthurs Memorial Library, Brookville, PA

The Rebecca M. Arthurs Memorial Library was one of the recipients of the 2011 Dollar General/YALSA Grant for summer reading programs. The library used the $1,000 grant to fund a reading incentive program using the 2011 CLSP theme "You Are Here," plus an author visit, programming to introduce teens to cultural diversity, and to provide teens with an opportunity to create and present programs at the library. The program for teens in grades 7-12 ran from late June to mid-August. Teens were encouraged to read books from YALSA reading lists, especially books set in different cultures, and they could earn weekly incentives. The library purchased up-to-date materials to support the summer reading curriculum of cultural diversity. The program was run by the Teen Book Club leader, the project coordinator, and volunteers.

MAKE WAVES @ YOUR LIBRARY TWEEN & TEEN SUMMER READING PROGRAM; YOU ARE HERE TWEEN & TEEN SUMMER READING PROGRAM

Olathe (Kans.) Public Library

The Olathe Public Library ran its summer reading incentive programs in 2010 and 2011, using the CLSP themes, for 6-12 graders.. The programs were conducted online at www.oplteens.org. Teens registered at the website and logged on to record their reading hours, registering for a grand prize drawing. Teens could also log their hours at the Olathe Library. For every 400 pages or four hours of reading completed (up to 4,800 pages or forty-eight hours), teens could claim a prize, including earbuds, Chick-fil-A coupons, Red Robin Monster Milkshake coupons, and so on. Every teen who reached sixteen hours or 1,600 pages won a free paperback book.

Teens could also win incentives for submitting reviews—each review qualified teens for a weekly prize drawing. Prizes included tickets to Major League Baseball games in Kansas City, waterpark passes, passes to local pools, and similar items.

Teens who won prizes were notified by library staff and could pick the prizes up at either of Olathe's two branches. Review prizes were first-come, first-served.

In addition to the incentive program, the library provided craft, science, and babysitting programs with refreshments.

The library used its YA programming budget (its annual budget is $3,500); a Comcast grant to cover printing, advertising, and books; funds from the Friends of the Library to cover prize and incentive money; and funds from Wal-Mart to cover costs of materials for such programs as the babysitting classes. The total amount spent was approximately $4,000 for the 2010 program. There were no costs beyond staff time to set up the online program.

More than 500 teens participated in the 2010 program, and the library received no complaints that it was online. Young Adult Librarian Angela Parks said that the Teen Library Club and the tween and teen volunteers helped plan and execute the program in 2010. For 2011, they made a few minor changes to the program in regards to counting minutes versus hours and having email addresses verified. The most significant problem from the 2010 program was teens entering incorrect email addresses.

READ GREEN! READ, RELAX, REWARD— TEEN SUMMER READING CLUB
Washington-Centerville Library, Centerville, OH

In 2009, the Washington-Centerville Library ran its Teen Summer Reading Club as a paperless program. Tweens and teens entering sixth grade through graduating twelfth grade could join the eight-week program at both the Centerville and Woodbourne branches of the library and online. Other than being paperless, the TSRC was a traditional reading incentive program: teens could read eight books in the eight weeks, and for each completed book they could enter the grand prize drawing. More than 1,000 teens participated and read 8,499 books. Approximately two-thirds of the teens who completed the evaluation ranked the TSRC as "awesome."

The TSRC received $2,100 from library funding and spent it on prizes for the weekly prize drawings (gift cards from Borders, Starbucks, and Target), the grand prize (an iPod Touch), contest prizes, and refreshments for programs. The program spent approximately $500 on commercial printing expenses for community and school information sheets, flyers, and posters, and $84 for two vinyl posters came out of the general library publication fund. Three full-time teen staff, one graphic designer, one systems department staffer, one webmaster, and a community relations manager (who approved the theme, contests, flyers, and so on) worked on the program. The library hired four college students to be reading club assistants in the libraries; they packaged incentives, weekly prizes, and called the winners throughout the summer program.

The librarians researched TSRC ideas online, they researched green concepts to generate ideas for contests, used library reference books to create contest questions, and created a teen booklist featuring green titles, such as *Saving the Planet* by Gail Gauthier and *Earthgirl* by Jennifer Cowan. They relied heavily on the 40 Developmental Assets for Adolescents from the Search Institute as they planned, executed, and evaluated the program. Planning for the TSRC began in December, when the kids', teens' and adult clubs met to choose the general theme. Brainstorming program and contest ideas began in January, and all programs and contests were finalized by May 1 for publication in the library's Calendar of Events. In January, the librarians also met with the graphic designer to create the logo, templates, and web pages. In February, the systems department joined in to discuss the TSRC database content. The librarians started contacting local businesses for donations in March; fourteen teen-friendly businesses donated 1,351 incentives for a total value of $10,657.93. In May, librarians met with the local schools' media center directors and presented information and program handouts for distribution to students and parents.

The general structure of the program remains the same every year, with only the theme and accompanying logo and graphics changing. The one change the librarians made for the next year was that teens must read at least eight books in the eight weeks of the program to receive a single entry into the grand prize drawing. They can still get weekly prizes through the weekly drawings and other smaller prizes for winning the various contests.

BOOK DISCUSSION GROUP RAFFLES
Mary L. Stephens Branch, Yolo County Library, Davis, CA

Reference Librarian/Teen Specialist Deatra Cohen uses book reviews and book discussion groups paired with raffles to encourage teen participation in the library's summer reading programs. Teens submit a review for each book they read; each review is worth three raffle tickets toward the bucket prizes at the end of the summer. She offers several book discussion groups over the summer; she chooses the books, provides several copies, then has teens sign up for the discussions. Typically, fifteen to twenty teens attend. Every time a teen participates in the discussion by asking a question, answering a question, or commenting on the book, the teen receives a raffle ticket. The more they participate in the discussion, the more raffle tickets they can earn for the end of the summer raffles. They're called bucket raffles because that's what the teens wanted. Cohen uses paper bags for "buckets," and labels each bag with the possible prize a teen can win. The teens can put their raffle tickets into any bucket, they can put all into one, or spread them out among any desirable prizes. The grand prize drawing was an iPod and other prizes included movie tickets. At the end of summer reading party, Cohen would draw winners from each bag.

ACTIVITY PROGRAMS

One sure-fire way to bring teens and tweens into the library over the summer is to host fun, engaging activities connected to a summer reading theme. While many libraries adopt the nationwide theme selected each year by the Collaborative Summer Library Program (CSLP; www.cslpreads. org), many also choose to use their own theme or host events in addition to using the CSLP theme. The programs listed here are successful examples from libraries across the United States and include information on program length, costs, targeted age groups, and recommended resources. The listed programs are a mix of those relating to a CSLP theme or an independent theme and include special one-off events, passive programming, writing workshops, and more.

GET MEDIEVAL
New Braunfels (Texas) Public Library

Planning started at New Braunfels in early spring; the librarians proposed a budget to the Friends of the Library for funding, which approved the $3,000 budget. The library held a lunch for school librarians in April, at which they introduced the program and handed out posters and flyers for their libraries. Librarian Kit Ward-Crixell worked with the Teen Advisory Group to plan events and create a bibliography of medieval themed fiction and nonfiction. The library had a Kick-off Day for the program with sword fighting knights—Jousting Knights and Steeds of the Texas Renaissance Festival, a bagpiper (the library hired a local college student), and sign-up tables so teens could pick up their reading logs.

The other programs emphasized teen participation, as they built and fired water balloon launching trebuchets, learned the basics of sword fighting, made herbal soap, created coats of arms, and built a cardboard castle. The last program was a catered banquet of authentic medieval foods. These events were spread out during the weeks that school was out for summer on different days of the week to accommodate as many schedules as possible.

Ward-Crixell used nonfiction resources *Design Your Own Coat of Arms* by Rosemary Chorzempa and *Backyard Ballistics* by William Gurstelle, and she found herbal soap recipes online. One full-time staff person implemented the program (Ward-Crixell), aided by the teen advisory group, who helped with the soap making and trebuchet programs. The library paid $1,400 for the jousters, which accounted for almost half the program's budget. Ward-Crixell said that the program can be done inexpensively if a library only focuses on purchasing materials to make the various projects. The popular cardboard box construction day (to build the castle) was the cheapest program in terms of cost vs. popularity.

The library isn't very big; the previous year's summer program attracted around twenty-five teens, and "Get Medieval" brought in more than one hundred to sign up.

YOU ARE HERE

Rebecca M. Arthurs Memorial Library, Brookville, PA

Using a $1,000 grant from the Dollar General Literacy Foundation and YALSA, the library put together a slate of special cultural programming for it 2011 program, "You Are Here." The library brought YA author Beth Fantaskey to speak to the teens, and it was able to offer one-on-one time with her for any of the teens who participated in the summer reading program. The library also did programs offering crafts and foods

QUICK GAMES

Inspired by *Minute to Win It*, a game show that ran on NBC in 2011, libraries can encourage teens to participate in these quick game challenges. All of these games involve teens using household objects and take less than a minute to complete. Cluster the games together as a challenge, with stations. The teens who complete the most stations can win a prize.

This Blows: Each teen needs to blow up a balloon and use the air in the balloon to blow fifteen plastic cups off from a table. The balloon can be blown up as many times as necessary to accomplish the task in sixty seconds.

Bottoms Up : Teens must knock six cans off of six different tables with a yo-yo that is attached to the player's waist with a belt and hangs down the player's back side. The player must use body momentum to swing the yo-yo to knock down the six cans in 60 seconds. This game requires a large open space because it's hard to control the yo-yo from behind oneself.

Johnny Applestack: Teens must stack apples end-on-end to create a tower that is five apples high. The tower must remain standing for three seconds.

Mega Bubble Challenge Give teens a bottle of bubbles with a wand. Each player needs to blow bubbles and move one across the room by blowing on it. The player must move a bubble from one part of the room to the other and through a large ring, such as a hula hoop. It's quite a challenge, because the player needs to blow a bubble that is dense enough to move across the room, and it can't be blown too high in the air or it can't be controlled.

Save the Joker: Stack five full decks of cards on five glass soda bottles, with a Joker at the bottom of each stack. The player must blow all of the cards off of the bottle except the last card, which is the joker. If the player blows too hard, the whole deck will blow off; if the player doesn't blow hard enough, nothing happens. The player gets five tries to achieve the challenge in sixty seconds.

Moving On Up: This challenge uses thirty-nine large plastic cups of the same color and one cup of the same style in a different color. Stack the forty cups with the odd color on the bottom.

The object of the game is to move each of the thirty-nine cups to the bottom of the stack, which will move the position of the odd colored cup, using alternating hands, and getting the odd color cup back to its original place at the bottom, in sixty seconds.

Defying Gravity: The player must keep three inflated balloons in the air for sixty seconds, without holding them or letting them rest on the body, or letting them hit the ground. This is actually a lot more difficult than it seems.

Stack Attack: The player must stack thirty-six plastic cups into a a pyramid and then back into a single stack.

from countries such as Greece, Africa, the Philippines, and France. The program was designed to introduce cultural diversity to the library's rural teens in a way to make it real and meaningful to them in their daily lives and help them to appreciate the world beyond their local community. The library also planned to provide a webcam to allow the teens to talk with teens from elsewhere—another country or another state. Weekly one-hour sessions included the crafts and foods.

READ GREEN! READ, RELAX, REWARD
Washington-Centerville Public Library, Centerville, OH

Washington-Centerville Public Library's 2009 Teen Summer Reading Club included "green" themed contests and ten programs. Every week, the library held Totally Teen Tuesdays (TTT), which alternated between bingo nights and open video game nights, including *Guitar Hero, Rock Band, Dance Dance Revolution, Super Smash Bros. Brawl,* and others. The library raffled off donated prizes at each TTT. The library also held the Teen Green Swap Meet, in which teens donated gently used unwanted items and received a credit to redeem at the swap meet. The library also held four contests, both on paper and online:
- A true/false quiz with "green" facts
- endangered animals identification

- fill-in-the-black using "green" words
- and a word scramble featuring "green" products.

Contest winners received iTunes, Tropical Smoothie, Panera, or GameStop gift cards. Several teens also received consolation prizes from Coldstone Creamery and Extra Innings (a local batting cage).

YOU ARE HERE

Bay County Library, Panama City, FL

Bay County Library's Youth Services Department in Panama City, FL used the "You Are Here" theme for its overall teen summer reading theme, but it focused more attention on its Teen Tuesdays weekly programs throughout the six-week-long program. Each Tuesday at 2 p.m., Youth Services offered a craft program, ranging from duct tape wallets to origami to steampunk crafts. Volunteers ran the origami program and helped with the steampunk crafts. The department photocopied instruction sheets for eight origami designs. Ten tweens and teens came to the program and folded paper cups, samurai helmets, flapping birds, paper balloons, and a sequence of designs from a house to a piano to a fox finger puppet, as well as the five-fold Origami Yoda from Tom Angleberger's novel, *The Strange Case of Origami Yoda*. That design is actually featured in the second book, *Darth Paper Strikes Back*.

The steampunk crafts program began with a team building contest; YA specialist Tania Watts grouped teens into four teams and gave each team a box of spaghetti noodles and a bag of marshmallows. The teams were given ten minutes to build a structure with the spaghetti and marshmallows, and at the end of the time, the team who managed to build the tallest structure that could stand for three minutes won. Watts talked briefly about the library's collection of YA steampunk fiction and provided a booklist. She brought out a box of old bicycle inner tubes that had been donated by a local bike shop. She had purchased several fun, funky, old-fashioned buttons and buckles and had needle, thread, and Krazy Glue. The teens could make things like rings, wristbands, armbands, and one boy made a belt. They could glue or sew the different geegaws onto their creations. One teenage boy, who had never picked up a needle and thread in his life, made a wristband and sewed several buttons on. Volunteers brought all kinds of industrial-looking charms and beads, along with jewelry findings,

FOOD PROGRAMS

Teens love to eat, and food programs are a fine activity to include in summer reading programming! Hosting a food program does not need to be messy or even require a kitchen. Read on for some simple ideas to get teens eating at your library this summer.

Candy Sushi

Many libraries host candy sushi programs, particularly with the anime club; tips here come from YALSA's YA-YAAC email discussion list (http://lists.ala.org/sympa/info/ya-yaac). Most candy sushi use rice Krispie treats, and most librarians will buy pre-packaged versions, which have to be flattened to roll the "sushi." Several librarians suggested flattening the treats while still in the package to reduce the sticky mess. With the pre-packaged treats, one treat and one fruit roll-up will make one roll of candy sushi. Teens can use Swedish fish, sour orange gummy slices, green gummy slices, Skittles, M&Ms and other kinds of candy to create their sushi. Chocolate sauce can take the place of soy sauce. Looking for recipes? Try these sites:

- http://candy.about.com/od/candybasics/ss/candysushi_sbs.htm
- www.foodnetwork.com/recipes/sare-moulton/candy-sushi-recipe/index.html
- www.wikihow.com/Make-Candy-Sushi (this has a video demo)

Make Your Own Pocky

Pocky is a Japanese candy-coated cracker snack that is popular with teens, and it's fairly easy to make your own. You'll need microwaveable chocolate (chips or wafers), cracker sticks, paper plates, wax paper, and a microwave. Melt some of the chocolate on a paper plate, then roll a cracker stick around in it, coating the cracker up to about an inch or so from the end so fingers don't end up coated in chocolate. If the teens don't eat up all the homemade pocky before they dry, lay the coated crackers on some wax paper and freeze for 5-15 minutes. You must use wax paper (or aluminum foil), because the chocolate will stick to the paper plates.

and helped teens make earrings, necklaces, bracelets, and bookmarks. One teen brought a large gear he had found on the road, which he had cleaned up and put on a chain. He took some of the wire and wove it with beads and charms onto the gear. The program was only supposed to run for an hour, but the teens all stayed until almost 4 p.m., determined to finish their creations.

BOREDOM BUSTERS
Mission Viejo (Calif.) Library

Some libraries have not been able to hold programs for teens because of budget reductions, but some of the librarians at those libraries offer passive programs. Allison Tran, Teen Services Librarian at Mission Viejo Library created Boredom Busters in 2011, a make-and-take crafts program. She ran a four-week Summer Reading Program, and she provided a different international or travel-themed craft each week: origami, a matchbox Louvre, tropical vacation marble magnets, and mini scrapbooks. Craft examples, including photos, can be found at Tran's blog at http://reading-everywhere.blogspot.com/search/label/summer%20reading.

STUDIO SCRAWL
West Windsor Branch, Mercer County Library System, Princeton Junction, NJ

The West Windsor Branch of the Mercer County Library System held "Studio Scrawl," a series of six writing workshops for tweens and teens 11–18 years old (entering sixth through twelfth grade) during the library system's six week Summer Reading Program. Each week, a professional writer led a workshop on a different topic:

- Playwriting
- Character Development
- The Art of the Short, Short Story
- Sportswriting
- Songwriting
- Poetry

The length of each workshop depended on the individual presenter's estimate of the time needed to cover the topic. For the songwriting workshop, the presenter brought in a laptop to write the lyrics, substitute for percussion instruments, and to record the final song.

Young Adult Librarian Carolyn Aversano decided to create "Studio Scrawl" because a number of teens had expressed an interest in writing programs. She tried to create a series of workshops that would be fun and wouldn't feel like school. She reached out to New Jersey authors whose books circulated well in the branch library, the Delaware Valley Poets (a central New Jersey–based group of poets), sports reporters she knew from a previous career, and to her Head of Reference, who was also a playwright. She started making contacts with possible presenters in late March, and made the schedule on a "first contacted, first scheduled" basis. She then created flyers and a program poster. Because she wasn't sure how popular the workshops would be, she issued tickets to participants upon registration. Registration sheets and tickets were available two weeks prior to each workshop. She sent reminder emails to participants four to six days before the workshop, and she made reminder calls two days prior to each workshop. Every participant received a "notebook" – a few pieces of copy paper between a front notebook cover and a piece of cardstock for a back cover—and a Q&A NJ pen. At each workshop, participants were asked to write their email address on the back of their ticket, and Aversano kept a spreadsheet record of the email addresses with the corresponding workshops attended. She used SurveyMonkey to create an online survey and sent emails with a link to the survey, asking Studio Scrawl attendees to complete the survey within three weeks.

Aversano only had to hire the leader for the Songwriting workshop. The Playwriting presenter was a library staff member, and the two YA authors, the poet, and the sports journalist all volunteered to conduct the workshops. The total cost for Studio Scrawl was $300. Aversano set a limit of fifteen attendees for each workshop; five of the six workshops had fifteen participants registered, twelve or thirteen actually attended each one.

Based on the responses to her survey, Aversano scheduled several Studio Scrawl workshops during the school year. Two workshops on the College Application Essay were scheduled in the Fall 2010; both were

PROGRAMMING WITH NO BUDGET

Your library has no budget, and you can't approach local businesses for donations. Wondering what to do? The following low- or no-cost ideas came from the YA-YAAC email discussion list. Librarians who post to it are willing to share their ideas, so join the discussion at http://lists.ala.org/sympa/info/ya-yaac to find even more simple, fun program ideas for your library.

No-sew t-shirt pillows
Ask the teens to bring in one of their old, clean t-shirts. They can cut two equal squares from the shirt (generally they can cut off the arms and the very top of the shirt, and cut off the hem right above the stitching), then cut strips about an inch apart, about an inch and a half long. They can tie the strips from the front and back pieces together. Stuffing can be strips of old sheets, used dryer sheets (start saving them up months in advance and ask staff members to save theirs for you), clean old socks, torn up old towels, and so on. Teens can glue or sew on decorations such as bits of lace and other trims, patches, buttons, and so on(ask staff members, teens' parents to donate) or use fabric markers to decorate the pillows.

Cubee Crafts
Cubees are make-it-yourself paper toys that do not require glue, tape, or other adhesives. The library can find designs to print out using plain white card stock and a color printer (Cubee Craft, www.cubeecraft.com, offers free, downloadable designs featuring pop culture characters and more). Librarians who have done this advise pre-cutting the slots to prevent accidents with X-acto knives.

Beach Ball Sports
Use empty water bottles to set up bowling pins, using a beach ball as the bowling ball. Teens can also play volleyball with beach balls. It's a good way to burn off teen energy.

Checkers Tournaments
Using checkerboards owned by the library (or donated by staff of volunteers), set up a quickie round-robin style tournament. Prizes could be snack-size candy bars.

Scary Stories Open Mic

Find and distribute YA titles that make for good read-aloud spooky stories. Let the teens take turns reading in their best spooky voice. Teens can also make up their own stories (the more nonsensical the better) or tell stories they've heard elsewhere.

Community Speakers

Some libraries have been able to attract government employees with interesting jobs—think the county coroner or a crime scene investigator—to speak about their work and some of the interesting cases they have had. Consider the loocal animal rescue organization, as a rescue dog handler might be willing to give a talk to teens.

full, so a third workshop was scheduled for March 2011. Another Studio Scrawl was scheduled with a YA author for Teen Tech Week.

TEEN MYSTERY NIGHT

La Vista (Neb.) Public Library

Teen Mystery Night is the biggest teen event in La Vista Public Library's Summer Reading Programs since 2009. Teen Coordinator Lindsey Tomsu created Teen Mystery Night to encourage teens to participate in an interactive mystery game (similar to mystery dinner theater) where they get to actively solve a mystery. The program is open to everyone ages 11 to 18. Twenty-four teens attended the first mystery night in 2009 and forty-one attended in 2010. Tomsu estimated that fifty teens would attend; the program has been increasingly popular over the years. Each Mystery Night is held from 6 to 8 p.m. in the library's large meeting room, which can accommodate 200 people.

The teen librarian in charge has needed to recruit other library staff to help set up the room about two hours prior to the event; no teen volunteers could be used because they wanted to play and could therefore not be allowed an advance peek at the mystery.

Tomsu ordered teen mystery kits (www.janetdickey.com) to set up her crime-solving interactive game. The kits provide all the elements one needs to run the mystery night except for props. When the teens arrive, they receive the detective's guides, which explain the set-up of the mystery and give important information about the victim, suspect statements, and so on. The guide also contains the answer sheet that each teen needs to fill out. They must investigate three scenes—a crime scene, an ancillary scene, and the chief detective's office—and search for clues to help them answer four questions: who did it, why did they do it, how did they do it, and what evidence do you have to support your conclusions. After the teens investigate all three scenes in a set order of progression), they are allowed time to answer the questions while they enjoy snacks. Once everyone has given the librarian the answer sheets, she "grades" them. The two teens who come closest to answering all questions correctly win prizes. After the winners are announced, the librarian goes through all four answers and explains the solution.

Tomsu detailed her procedure she follows each year:

1. Order a mystery kit. The kit contains a program guide showing all the steps involved in hosting the event, the detective's guide, the evidence folder with the clues that need to be planted at the scenes, and crime scene tape.

2. Read through the program guide. It explains all the steps needed to implement the program. The first priority is to make a registration sheet, make posters to advertise the program, and then make the clues, using the directions given. Next, you need to think about the scenes you have to create. The more realistic they are, the better. Suggestions for additional props are given in the program guide; bring props from home and ask your co-workers.

3. The day of the event, set up the scenes two hours prior to the event. Give plenty of space between each scene to accommodate groups of teens milling about.

4. Use the crime scene tape around the actual "crime scene" and also outside the room in which the event is taking place. Tomsu said that during her first Teen Mystery Night, patrons were asking what happened, thinking a real crime had taken place.

5. Have the teens check in to know how many people are attending. Have them sit down at tables where pencils and their detective guides are placed. Once everyone has checked in and sat down, begin the game by following the outline given in the program guide.

6. After all scenes are investigated and all answer sheets are handed in and graded, announce the winners, give the prizes, and then explain the solution to the gams.

7. Success of the program will vary; Tomsu suggests basing it on how many teens usually come to programs. Her first mystery night was held when she came into the job in the middle of the summer, and the planned events were getting fewer than ten teens at each event. That mystery night was her very first program that she planned and implemented herself, and twenty-four teens attended. During the 2010 SRP, her programs averaged twenty to thirty teens each, and her mystery night attracted more than forty teens. For her library, these are very successful programs.

Tomsu has been able to run the mystery night programs on her own except for needing one person to help her set up the room and crime scenes. Also, she needs a volunteer to lie down on the floor so the other person can make a masking tape "chalk" outline of them. Her teen attendees usually stay to help clean up after the program. She does suggest additional help to take pictures and supervise the teens.

The program is fairly low cost, especially in comparison to how many teens have attended her mystery nights. For each mystery, Tomsu used props from the library, such as books and magazines, office supplies, a globe, a desk, etc. Tomsu purchased inexpensive refreshments at a local market, and each winner received a $5 gift card to Borders and one large movie theater-size candy item. Her total cost for fifty teens was $70.

TEEN DIGITAL CAMERA SCAVENGER HUNT
Watonwan County Library, St. James, MN

The Watonwan County Library annually holds this program for teens ages 12 to 19. The scavenger hunt runs about two and a half hours. Teens must bring their own digital cameras or camera phones for the program. Assistant Director Stacy Lienemann proposed the program to the library's teen advisory group, who voted to include it in the summer's programming.

The main part of the planning is creating a list of 100 items that teens must find and take pictures of, with at least one person from the team in the photo. Depending on what items were selected, Lienemann contacted different community members and businesses who could help the teens find the items on the list or serve as items themselves. On the day of the scavenger hunt, teens would come to the library in their teams and Lienemann would quickly run through the rules: someone from the team must be in the photo, all team members must start at the library together and arrive at the library before the deadline with their camera, all items must be visible in the photo, all team members must ask permission for taking anyone's photo, a team member must describe each photo for the library staff member running the program, all photos must be on the same camera, but multiple items can be in one photo (this rule was made so that teams couldn't split up). The teams would each get their list of 100 items and then head out to find and photograph everything. The scavenger hunt list has included such items as:

- an anthill,
- a non-group member throwing a ball or Frisbee,
- someone wearing polka dots,
- a group photo of everyone crossing a street,
- something to do with *Twilight* that isn't a book or movie/DVD,
- a birthday card specifically for a 13-year-old, moss,
- and other such items.

Some items, such as newspapers, yearbooks, teen event signs, CDs, and the like are in the library. When the teams returned to the library, they explained to Lienemann what they had in each photo. She awarded prizes and asked the teens to complete a simple evaluation form.

Lienemann said the program is easy, because the teens leave the library to take their photos, and she's the only staff member needed to go through the photos and check off all the list items. Because the teens use their own cameras, the cost of the program is low. She spent $30 mailing postcards out to teens for whom she didn't have email addresses. The first year, she spent $15 on prizes, but in subsequent years, local businesses and sports teams have donated prizes (such as WNBA tickets or movie theater passes). The program comes out of the library's programming budget.

TEEN FEST
El Paso (TX) Public Library System

Teen Fest is the annual kick-off event for the Teen Summer Reading Club of the El Paso Public Library System. It takes place at Cohen Stadium in El Paso at the start of the TSRC. The program lasts about six hours, from noon to 6 p.m. The event is aimed at the teens, ages 13 to 18, but everyone is welcome to attend. The afternoon includes a car show, more than ten local bands, booths set up by local businesses and community organizations, educators, health professionals, local authors, artisans, and local colleges. Teens register for the TSRC, they can play games, do crafts, and get free books. In 2005, the kickoff's first year, seventy-five teens attended; in 2011, about 5,000 people attended.

Carmen Hernandez of El Paso Public Library System organizes the event each year; she works with the fifteen members of the El Paso Public Library's Teen Hangout Committee to solicit donations from local businesses and conduct fundraising events throughout the year. More than twenty-five library staff and volunteers work at the event itself. The program starts with $2,400 seed money from the TSRC budget; this pays for the band sound system, t-shirts with the Teen Fest logo, crafts, supplies, and so on. The committee solicits $25 from branch's Friends group to pay for the staff lunch.

The El Paso Public Library puts on the Teen Fest every year because the library wants teens to connect to their community, and see everything the community has to offer. Community groups currently receive free booths, but the library is considering requesting donations to help cover costs.

CAMP HALF BLOOD
Springfield (Vt.) Town Library

In 2010, the Springfield Town Library held a two-day program for tweens and young teens entering sixth through ninth grades called Camp Half Blood, based on the Percy Jackson and the Olympians series by Rick Riordan. On the first day, participants listened to a read-aloud of a segment of *The Lightning Thief* by Rick Riordan. They were then given directions and sent on a scavenger hunt activity called "The Quest for a

Lightning Bolt." A prize (a sword pen) was given to each participant who successfully completed the hunt and returned with a bookmark shaped like a lightning bolt. On the second day, participants watched the DVD of *The Lightning Thief* movie. Refreshments similar to food described in the book were served at both events.

Children's Librarian Cheryl Cox found guidance by reading Riordan's books, Greek mythology books, and websites such as www.rickriordan.com/my-books/percy-jackson/resources/teachers-guide.aspx and www.hyperionbooksforchildren.com. She planned the program, set the date, ordered the prizes and materials for the program, and advertised it using signs, blogs, handouts, calendars, emails, news articles, and public access television. She shopped for and prepared the food herself. The Friends of the Springfield Town Library provided financial support. Some of the food, the sword pens, and some materials (leather cording, wooden beads, and gold coins) cost about $35, and Cox purchased the DVD ($19) for the library with her audio-visual budget. The movie license is provided by the Vermont Department of Libraries at no extra cost to the library.

The participants enjoyed the program. Cox said one teen told his grandmother that he wished Cox was his teacher, something she said she considers a major compliment. If she were to repeat the program, she would add a third session.

PARKOUR

Puyallup (Wash.) Public Library

The Puyallup Public Library hosted a parkour workshop in summer 2011. Parkour involves efficient movement across obstacles found in most places; examples can be seen in the opening of *Casino Royale*, the James Bond film starring Daniel Craig, or the French film *District B-13*. Instructors from an organization called Parkour Visions, based in Seattle, taught the workshop to twenty teens ages thirteen to eighteen, with many spectators looking on. This program is best done outdoors; the library is located near a park, with wide open spaces and a series of cement blocks designed to look like books.

The program focused more on fitness and safety, and instructors did not let any of the participants perform wild and crazy stunts. The instructors took the teens through a series of stretches to warm up, and then began jumping drills. They used the cement blocks to teach the teens how to jump from one to the other and to land quietly. At the park's bandstand, the teens were shown other moves, such as using the railing, corners, ledges, and steps; all the while, the instructors kept reminding them about being safe while moving, moving at their own pace, and only doing the moves they felt comfortable doing. The instructors also talked about improving one's balance, using the example of standing on one foot while brushing one's teeth and then closing the eyes to make it more difficult. Young Adult Librarian Bonnie Svitavsky helped the instructors stand as guards for teens who wanted to try to walk along a rail going up a sloping ramp; they stood on either side of the teens and offered hands to balance them. The instructors made sure the teens did more stretching to cool down, then talked about being respectful of property and answered questions. Libraries who want to do a Parkour program should make sure they're not doing it in the very height of summer, and they'll want to provide lots of water to keep the participants hydrated because of the physical exertion. This program brought in teen boys Svitavsky had never seen come to the library before.

The library contracted with Parkour Visions for a cost of $10 per teen, which was a discounted price. The Friends of the Puyallup Public Library paid for the program. Each teen participant had to turn in a permission slip signed by a parent or guardian.

TEENS' TOP TEN ACTIVITY IDEAS

YALSA's Teens' Top Ten is designed for libraries to encourage summer reading. Each year, YALSA releases the list of twenty-five nominees at www.ala.org/teenstopten for librarians to use during summer reading programs. Teens can read the books throughout the summer and vote in August and September at the Teens' Top Ten website to choose their favorite books. The following replicable program ideas are adapted from the TTT Toolkit (see Appendix C and the Teens' Top Ten website (www .ala.org/teenstopten) for more ideas from the toolkit.

PROGRAMMING IDEAS

Work with the library's Teen Advisory Group (TAG) to brainstorm, plan and implement activities to promote the summer reading program and to draw readers into the library by planning regular events during their summer vacation. Find information on staffing a TAG at the YALSA Wiki for more information (http://wikis.ala.org/yalsa/index.php/Teen_Advisory_Groups).

The library's summer reading programs are an ideal time to introduce the nominated Teens' Top Ten titles. The books that have been nominated by teens across the country should appeal to the young adult audience that the library is already targeting, making reading during the summer more enticing.

Consider collaborating with local organizations and businesses to hold some of the events outside the library at schools, community centers, shopping malls, coffee shops and other places teens in the community hang out. Branching out into the community will help reach more teens than those who already frequent the library. It could be as simple as a small display advertising the program and events, or as elaborate as regular parties held just for teens.

For more programming ideas or to add ideas, visit the YALSA wiki at http://wikis.ala.org/yalsa/index.php/Ideas_for_Using_the_Teens%27_Top_Ten.

Book Campaign Contest

WHAT THE LIBRARY NEEDS:

- Teens will need access to art supplies

Cost: $0.50 - $1 per poster board (if providing poster board)

Have teens create campaign posters of their favorite TTT books. Teens should include reasons why other teens should vote for the titles on the posters. The posters can be displayed in the teen area during the week teens vote for their favorite books to generate interest in the actual voting.

Book Cover Contest

WHAT THE LIBRARY NEEDS:

- Teens will need access to a camera or art supplies

Cost: Free

Hold an art and photography contest for teens to design a new cover for their favorite nominated title. Participants could send the photo electronically or create their art and submit it at the library. Display covers in your teen area to generate further interest in TTT. Judging could be done by staff, a local "celebrity" panel, or the general public. Personalize our sample entry form.

The art could be auctioned off to raise funds to support additional teen programming at the library.

Another similar option is to have teens create campaign posters of their favorite TTT books. Teens should include reasons why other teens should vote for the titles on the posters. The posters can be displayed in the teen area during the week teens vote for their favorite books to generate interest in the actual voting.

Book Talks/Book Reviews

WHAT THE LIBRARY NEEDS:

(If recording the book talks as podcasts, participants will need to have the following available to them.)

- Computer with an Internet connection
- Microphone
- An audio editing program (GarageBand from Apple, Adobe's Audition, or Audacity) to record the podcast.
- A VoIP program, such as Skype.

Cost: Free

Encourage teens to write book talks or book reviews for the books on the nominated list. These can then be recorded as a podcast, written on cards to display on the shelves next to the books, or posted on your library website. For book reviews, create a review form or reproduce the reading log from the toolkit at www.ala.org/teenstopten.

One way to help encourage teens is to have some type of raffle prize where teens must write a book talk or book review to get entered in the raffle. Prizes could be donated from local businesses. The library can also make certificates good for $1.00 off late fees, or a discount on books in a used book sale.

Book Trailers

WHAT THE LIBRARY NEEDS:

- Teens will need access to any of the resources listed below to create their book trailer. Please research the terms of use for each resource before recommending them to teens.

  - Windows Movie Maker (usually standard Windows software): http://www.microsoft.com/windowsxp/using/moviemaker/default.mspx
  - iMovie (usually standard Apple software): http://www.apple.com/ilife/imovie
  - Sprout Builder: http://sproutbuilder.com
  - Slideshow: http://www.slide.com/arrange
  - One True Media: http://www.onetruemedia.com
  - Photobucket: http://photobucket.com

Cost: Free

Encourage teens to create book trailers for the books on the nominated list. This could be done as a contest or just for fun. Include links to the book trailers on the library website.

Make sure you stress to teens that they need to use music and images in the public domain. Try Creative Commons search tool at http://search.creativecommons.org.

Double Score Summer Reading

WHAT THE LIBRARY NEEDS:

- Use the same method to track reading that the library otherwise uses

Cost: Free

An easy way to incorporate the Teens' Top Ten into an existing summer reading program is to encourage teens to read the nominated titles by letting them count those books as double. The library could also offer special prizes for those who choose to read the nominated books, or drawings from among the teens who have read them.

Literary Jeopardy

WHAT THE LIBRARY NEEDS:

- Slide show software
- Projector and a screen (or a blank wall)

Cost: Free

This quiz game could focus on the nominated titles specifically, or on literature in general. It could be done as a single event, perhaps part of the lock-in or as a series of contests to choose a final winner. Teens could sign up for the event individually or in teams.

To make the jeopardy game, write five or six questions and answers to each of the nominated titles. Then separate the titles to create five different games. Each book will be in its own category, with five or six categories per game. Put the questions for each category in order from easiest to most difficult and assign points accordingly, with 100 points for the easiest and 500 for the most difficult. Create the board with a slide show program and use a projector to display the board while you play. Staff can also try using www.jeopardylabs.com rather than slideshow software. There is nothing to download or register for. Staff could also go low-tech, and make the board on a blank wall or bulletin board using cardstock and tape.

Lookalike Contest

WHAT THE LIBRARY NEEDS:

- Digital camera
- Printer
- Bulletin board or poster board to display pictures

Cost: Free

Have teens dress up as the part of a character in one of the nominated titles. Use a digital camera to take a picture of each contestant, then print and post in the library. Teens can vote on who is the best lookalike. Alternatively, post the photos online and allow teens to vote electronically. Make sure to have a waiver for each participant before posting their pictures online.

Novel Soundtrack

WHAT THE LIBRARY NEEDS:

- A computer with Internet connection
- A location to share the playlist

Cost: Free

Teens create a soundtrack to follow a novel on the nominated list. Teens can create a free playlist at www.playlist.com. If teens need some inspiration for their playlist, send them to http://stepheniemeyer.com/index.html, for example. Once the playlist is complete, participants can post their playlist on Facebook, Twitter, or even to the library's blog. They can then listen to, and comment on each other's playlists. Check out YALSA's wiki for examples of books and authors with playlists and soundtracks.

An alternative to sharing the actual songs online would be to have the teens create their ideal playlist on paper and have that list on display with the nominated books. Create bookmarks listing the songs or artists submitted by teens.

Open Mic Soirée

WHAT THE LIBRARY NEEDS:

- Microphone
- Stage and seating areas
- Refreshments

Cost: $.50-$2 per person (for refreshments)

This is another event for teens to talk about their favorite books, including the nominated titles, with their peers. Simple to organize, all that's required is a microphone and a relaxed atmosphere. Teens could read a passage from their favorite book, or recite an original poem or song based on their favorite book.

Often teens are reluctant to perform in front of their peers, so consider recruiting a few excited volunteers to get things started.

Speed book sharing program

WHAT THE LIBRARY NEEDS:

- A bell or whistle to signal a partner change.
- Optional: Pencils and notepads could be provided by the library, and could be used as a marketing tool.

Cost: Free

This program is similar to speed dating, but instead of talking to each other about themselves, teens talk about their favorite books. Have the teens each find a partner to spend the first minute with. Each partner gets to talk about their favorite book for thirty seconds. Ring a bell or clap your hands when it's time to switch which partner is talking. After the first minute, teens find a new partner, and repeat until all of the teens have been partners once. Each of the participants will leave this activity with a list of titles recommended by their peers. The more teens participate, the more books they will learn about that they might be excited to read.

You're such a tease

WHAT THE LIBRARY NEEDS:

- Current Teens' Top Ten nominated books

Cost: Price of books, depending how many you order

Begin any teen program with a book teaser! Either booktalk one of the nominees or simply read the first chapter aloud to the group of teens. Read the first chapter or an excerpt from each nominee to pique teens' interest. Do this for twenty-five weeks or for each book that your library owns. Be sure to hand out flyers with the other nominees and voting information.

FOR MORE PROGRAMMING IDEAS

Participate in the Teens' Top Ten YALSA Librarians Group on Figment. com. This is a dedicated discussion group where librarians and library workers can come together to share materials and programming ideas for the TTT. The Figment.com editorial team will also share resources for the nominated titles, including author interviews, writing prompts, and other original programming. To join, simply create a free account on Figment and request membership to the YALSA group.

ALA Council Resolution on Ensuring Summer Reading Programs for All Children and Teens

WHEREAS, Libraries contribute to the intellectual growth of children and teens during the summer through reading programs; and

WHEREAS, ALA Policy 52.5.1 affirms that "the future of libraries and of society itself depends upon the preparedness of youth to carry adult responsibilities for business, government, parenthood and other leadership. Children and young adults cannot fulfill their potential or that of society without high quality library opportunities through both public and school libraries." and

WHEREAS, Summer Reading programs bring children and teens into the local library for reading and cultural activities; and

WHEREAS, Children and teens can benefit from summer programs that combine elements of youth development principles with academic enrichment; and

WHEREAS, Visiting their local library provides children with access to unlimited amounts of reading materials; and

WHEREAS, School and public librarians have cooperatively produced the summer reading lists to enhance both learning and recreation; and

WHEREAS, Studies of children's and teens' reading development cite the importance of extensive, successful reading experiences in the development of reading proficiency, most recently, IMLS/Dominican University study: Public Library Summer Reading Programs Close the Reading Gap; and

WHEREAS, Young library users will receive an opportunity to become lifelong readers and learners, by visiting the library frequently; now, therefore, be it

RESOLVED, That the American Library Association (ALA):

Urges Library Directors, Trustees, School Board members and supervising government bodies to insure that their libraries are provided adequate funding to ensure that their summer reading programs for all children and teens are maintained and that ALA promotes this resolution to all library systems and state boards of education in the country.

Adopted by the Council of the American Library Association
Monday, June 28, 2010
Washington, DC
Keith Michael Fiels
ALA Executive Director and ALA Council Secretary

ALA Library Fact Sheet 17: Summer Library Reading Programs

SUMMER READING PROGRAMS began in the 1890s as a way to encourage school children, particularly those in urban areas and not needed for farm work, to read during their summer vacation, use the library and develop the habit of reading.

THEMES

The American Library Association does not set the themes for summer reading programs held at many public libraries nationwide. These may be set by the individual library or by the state library. Many individual or state libraries use the themes set by the Collaborative Summer Library Program (CSLP; www.cslpreads.org), a grassroots consortium of states working together to provide high-quality summer reading program materials for children at the lowest cost possible for their public libraries.

GRANTS

The value of reading throughout the long summer vacation is recognized by the ALSC/BWI Reading Program Grant (www.ala.org/alsc/awards-grants/profawards/bookwholesalers), which is designed to encourage reading programs for children in a public library by providing financial assistance of $3,000, while recognizing ALSC members for outstanding program development. It is sponsored by BWI (Book Wholesalers, Inc.), and administered by the Association for Library Service to Children (ALSC, a division of ALA). Applications are due by December 1 of each year in support of a program the next summer.

BENEFITS

The benefits to readers in a summer reading program include:

- encouragement that reading become a lifelong habit
- reluctant readers can be drawn in by the activities
- reading over the summer helps children keep their skills up
- the program can generate interest in the library and books

And it being summer, the program can just be good fun and provide an opportunity for family time.

Talking points for the benefits of summer reading, Why Public Library Summer Reading Programs Are Important (http://dpi.wi.gov/pld/pdf/slp-points.pdf), have been made available by the Wisconsin Department of Public Instruction. A more comprehensive look on the topic, along with a bibliography, can be found on their web site at Research on the Importance of Summer Library Programs.

There are also public relations benefits of attracting new readers, maintaining or building a library presence in the community, and keeping or building traffic for the library. Over the years, many libraries have entered their summer reading program into the John Cotton Dana Library Public Relations Award (www.ebscohost.com/academic/john-cotton-dana), co-sponsored by The H.W. Wilson Company and ALA's Library Leadership and Management Association (LLAMA, a division of the American Library Association). For additional information on libraries and public relations, please see the Public Relations page on the ALA Professional

Tips Wiki (http://wikis.ala.org/professionaltips/index.php?title=Main_
Page#Advocacy_and_Public_Relations:).

RESEARCH

- McCombs, Jennifer Sloan, Catherine H. Augustine, Heather L.
  Schwartz, Susan J. Bodilly, Brian McInnis, Dahlia S. Lichter and
  Amanda Brown Cross. Making Summer Count: How Summer
  Programs Can Boost Children's Learning. Santa Monica, CA:
  RAND Corporation, 2011. Abstract and free eBook (PDF)
  version at http://www.rand.org/pubs/monographs/MG1120.
  Also available in print form.
  See the June 13, 2011 entry, First Comprehensive Research
  on Summer Slide Released, by Nora Fleming, on the Beyond
  School Blog of *Education Week* at http://blogs.edweek.org/
  edweek/beyond_schools/2011/06/first_comprehensive_research_
  on_summer_slide_released.html. Abstract excerpt: A review
  of the literature on summer learning loss and summer learning
  programs, coupled with data from ongoing programs offered by
  districts and private providers across the United States, demon-
  strates the potential of summer programs to improve achievement as well as the challenges in creating and maintaining such
  programs.
- "Prevent Summer Set Back" is a flier for parents which shares
  information on the benefits of summer reading. Published by
  the Colorado State Library and is available in both English
  (www.cslpreads.org/archive/PDF/school%20flyer%20_2_.pdf)
  and Spanish (www.cslpreads.org/archive/PDF/Spanish%20
  school%20flyer%20_2_.pdf).
- The National Center for Summer Learning (www.summerlearn-
  ing.org/), based at the Johns Hopkins University School of Education, offers some pertinent points as well as full text articles
  and abstracts on these pages.
- Highlights of Research on Summer Reading and Effects on
  Student Achievement (http://www.nysl.nysed.gov/libdev/summer/
  research.pdf: The New York Statewide Summer Reading Program
  created this 4 page bibliography of research sources.

- The Role of Public Libraries in Children's Literacy Development: An Evaluation Report (http://web.archive.org/web/20090107215714/http://www.statelibrary.state.pa.us/libraries/lib/libraries/Role%20of%20Libraries.pdf) by Drs. Donna Celano and Susan B. Neuman, Pennsylvania Library Association, 2001 (via the Internet Archive)
- Evaluating Summer Reading Programs: Suggested Improvements by Joe Matthews, Public Libraries Online (from July/August 2010 *Public Libraries,* www.publiclibrariesonline.org/magazines/featured-articles/evaluating-summer-reading-programs-suggested-improvements*).*
- The No Child Left Behind Summer Reading Achievers Program (http://www2.ed.gov/parents/academic/summer/reading/2004-index.html)was designed to encourage students in grades K-8 to read during the summer months and help prevent fall-off in reading skills during the vacation. Students who read 10 books over the summer received a variety of prizes, including free books and a Summer Reading Achievers certificate. Thousands of students at 11 sites nationwide benefited from the program. The outcomes of the program showed that with this program, participants showed no summer reading loss.
- Please see also the information provided about early literacy (http://wikis.ala.org/professionaltips/index.php/Early_Childhood_Literacy) for additional research supporting for children's summer reading programs.

View a list of additonal resources at the Summer Reading Programs page at the ALA Professional Tips Wiki (http://wikis.ala.org/professionaltips/index.php/Summer_Reading_Programs), including links to library summer reading programs and links to summer reading lists.

For more information on this or other fact sheets, contact the ALA Library Reference Desk by telephone: 800-545-2433, extension 2153; fax: 312-280-3255; e-mail: library@ala.org; or regular mail: ALA Library, American Library Association, 50 East Huron Street, Chicago, IL 60611-2795.

YALSA's Teens' Top Ten Toolkit

THE TEENS' TOP Ten (TTT) is a "teen choice" list of recommended reading, where teens nominate and choose their favorite books of the previous year. Nominators are members of teen book groups (YAGalley Groups) in fifteen school and public libraries around the country. Nominations are posted in April on Support Teen Lit Day, which is the Thursday of National Library Week. Teens across the country are encouraged to read as many nominees as they can during the summer. All interested readers aged twelve to eighteen can vote for their favorites online, anytime from mid August until mid September. The winners are announced via a webcast with special guests during Teen Read Week™ the third week of October.

> Please note: a full version of this toolkit, including downloadable graphics, is available at www.ala .org/teenstopten.

Ever since Teen Read Week (TRW) was inaugurated in 1998, many librarians have wanted to celebrate and encourage teen reading for more than just one week a year. In 2003, YALSA offered a chance for librarians to encourage teens to read, nominate, and vote for their ten favorite books of the year. More than 1,700 ballots were cast the first year, and that number has kept growing each year. More than 10,000 teens voted in 2011 for their favorite books!

GOAL

To get teens across the country to read all summer long, and then vote online for their favorites in August and September in preparation of the announcement of the winning titles during TRW in October. TTT also provides librarians with a resource to compliment their summer reading programming and services.

PROGRAM OVERVIEW

- Every two years, 15 libraries are selected to serve as a TTT nominating group. To be considered for the next round of groups, instructions on applying can be found at www.ala.org/teen-stopten.
- TTT books have wide appeal to teens between the ages of 12 and 18.
- Nominations are posted in April on Support Teen Lit Day, which is the Thursday of National Library Week.
- There are several ways that teens and librarians can participate:
    - Make sure that teens know where to find the nominations list and/or provide bookmarks/flyers with the list or a link to the list from your library's web site.
    - Add the titles to your collection and encourage other area libraries to add them to their collections.
    - Encourage teens/tweens to read the nominated books during the summer so that they can vote in August and September.
    - Promote the list to area public and school librarians by meeting with them or sending letters and postcards.
- Get your teens or Teen Advisory Groups to spread the word and vote!

- This event is sponsored by the Young Adult Library Services Association (YALSA).

TIMELINE

- *April:*
    - Nominations are announced and posted on YALSA's web site during National Library Week
    - Download the reading lists and bookmarks to display in the library
- *April–August*
    - Incorporate nominations into summer reading booktalks, programs and displays
- *August–September:*
    - Encourage teens to vote for their favorite titles at www.ala.org/teenstopten
- *Third week of October:*
    - Celebrate Teen Read Week™
    - Host an awards announcement party
- *Ongoing:*
    - Use TTT lists for collection development and readers' advisory

LAUNCH IDEAS

Summer Reading Programs:

Most public libraries implement summer reading clubs or programs for children and teens. The Teens' Top Ten nomination list provides a great resource for readers' advisory and encouraging your teens to read throughout the summer months.

Campaigns:

Public and school librarians can form partnerships to help promote teen reading throughout the summer. Work with your Teen Advisory Group (TAG) to brainstorm, plan and implement a special launch of your summer reading program. Some ideas to consider:

- Mail or email postcards and letters to help spread the word to librarians, teachers, school librarians, and area residents. Go to Get Publicity for ideas and sample letters. You can personalize them and place them on your library's letterhead!
- Conduct booktalks to English classes using the books on the nomination list, or have your teens create book trailers.
- Set up a table displaying the nominees in the cafeteria of local middle and high schools during their lunch periods. Hand out bookmarks with the reading list and flyers to promote your summer reading program. Provide small giveaways and hand out reading logs.
- Use your library's Web site, blog, social networking page, newsletter, etc. to promote the list and your summer programs. Include a link to the YALSA blog so teens can learn more about the nominated titles.
- Wear a button at work with the TTT logo that says "ask me who this year's nominees are!"

GET PUBLICITY

- Use communication tools at your disposal to launch the Teens' Top Ten nomination list and to promote specific events.
- Place information on the library's web site, blog and/or My Space page.
- Put flyers up in the library and throughout the local middle and high schools. Include information in the library's newsletter.
- Tailor the sample press release below and send it to your local newspaper.
- Spread the word to school teachers and area librarians with our sample letter. You can copy and paste the sample letter into your library's letterhead.

Sample Letters:

The following letters are examples to send to your local media and area librarians. Edit the letters with your library's information or tailor them to your needs. The sample press release can be sent to your public relations person/department to be distributed, or you can send it yourself to your local newspapers, publications, and television stations. The sample letter to teachers, school librarians, and area public librarians helps spread the word to local librarians that may not know about the Teens' Top Ten or that your library is promoting related events.

SAMPLE PRESS RELEASE

For Immediate Release

[insert date]

For more information contact:
[insert complete contact info, including phone # and email for the appropriate library personnel]

[insert headline in 18 pt. font]

Area teens are extending their reading beyond school this summer by taking part in their local teen summer reading program [insert name of program]. Every year in April since 2003, the Young Adult Library Services Association (YALSA) releases the list of nominees for the Teens' Top Ten List. Teens are encouraged to read the list of over 25 books to take part in voting for their ten favorite books of the year in August and September. The winning titles will be announced via a webcast during Teen Read Week in October.

[Insert current YALSA president's name here], YALSA's president, feels that "today's teens seem to have less and less free time, and there are increasingly more activities to for them to take part in during what little leisure time they have. That is why it's important to encourage teens to set aside some time to read." Literacy is a topic of both local and national concern, and falling test scores and lower graduation rates among teens today are a serious issue. Here in [insert name of home-town or state] standardized reading test scores for teens are [insert latest scores—check your state department of education's web site].

Studies show a regular reading habit makes teens better readers, and area librarian [insert full name of local librarian #1] agrees. [insert full name of local librarian #2] hopes to increase teen literacy locally by offering a series of programs for teens throughout [insert name of summer reading program]. Teens will be encouraged to read books that appeal to them from the Teens' Top Ten list. [describe the programs and provide contact information for readers who want to learn more]

Parents and caregivers of teens are encouraged to make time for their teens to read at home. [insert name of local librarian #2] offers these ideas:

- Visit the local public or school library with your teen to attend a program or to check out books or other reading materials.
- Set aside time each night for the family to read.
- Give books, audiobooks or magazine subscriptions to your teen as a gift or reward.
- Share your favorite book with your teen.
- Visit the Teens' Top Ten site at www.ala.org/teenstopten.
- Join or start a book discussion group at school or at the public library.

Teen Read Week™ is held annually during the third week of October. To find out more about the Teens' Top Ten and Teen Read Week contact your library at [insert local library contact info here].

SAMPLE LETTER TO TEACHERS & SCHOOL LIBRARIANS

Dear Teachers and School Librarians,

I am writing to ensure that you know about an exciting program for teens called the Teens' Top Ten (TTT), a "teens' choice" list where teens nominate and choose their favorite books of the previous year. Nominees are chosen by members of teen book groups from 15 school and public libraries around the country and are posted in April during National Library Week. Then, teens can vote for their favorite titles during August and September. The winning titles will be announced via webcast during Teen Read Week in October.

The Young Adult Library Services Association (YALSA) began the TTT program in 2003. Over 1,700 ballots were cast the first year, and in 2009 that number topped 11,000. The goal of TTT is to encourage teens across the country to read all summer long and then vote online for their favorites in October. **To reach that goal, we need your help**. Please help us with the following:

- Make sure that teens know where to find the nominations list (www.ala.org/teenstopten/) by providing bookmarks/flyers with the list or linking to the list from your web site.
- Add the titles to your collection or encourage students to visit the public library to get copies of the books.
- Encourage teens to read the nominated books during the summer so that they can vote during Teen Read Week.
- Remind your teens to vote at www.ala.org/teenstopten during the end of August and beginning of September.

For more information about the Teens' Top Ten program, please visit the website at www.ala.org/teenstopten/. If you'd like to know more about how we're celebrating at [insert name of your library here], or if you'd like to talk about ways we might partner to promote the TTT, please don't hesitate to get in touch with me. Thanks for all that you do to get more teens reading!

Sincerely,
[Enter your name & contact information here.]

SUSTAINING TEENS' INTEREST THROUGHOUT THE SUMMER

- Use Figment's free groups function to host your library's own private book club, where teens can discuss the books they're reading and where you can share information about your library's events and resources. You can also access and manage additional contests, writing prompts, games, and author interviews provided by Figment throughout the summer. Direct questions to: education@figment.com
- Feature a different TTT nominee each week via your library's Facebook page, Twitter, web site or in-library display.
- Create a bulletin board in your library or use Pinterest to have teens share their opinions about the TTT titles they read
- Create a grid with all of the TTT nominees listed so teens can check off which ones they've read. This can be a large, in-library grid, or small individual ones that teens can keep for personal use

Young Adults Deserve the Best: Competencies for Libraries Serving Youth

THE YOUNG ADULT Library Services Association (YALSA), a division of the American Library Association (ALA) that supports library services to teens, developed these competencies for librarians who serve young adults. Individuals who demonstrate the knowledge and skills laid out in this document will be able to provide quality library service for and with teenagers. Institutions seeking to improve their overall service capacity and increase public value to their community are encouraged to adopt these competencies.

YALSA first developed these competencies in 1981, which were revised in 1998, 2003, and 2010. The competencies can be used as a tool to evaluate and improve service, a foundation for library school curriculum, a framework for staff training and a set of guiding principles for use when speaking out for the importance of services to teens in libraries. Audiences for the competencies include:

- Library educators
- School and library administrators
- Graduate students

- Young adult specialists
- School librarians
- Library training coordinators
- Public library generalists
- Human resources directors
- Non-library youth advocates and service providers

Area I. Leadership and Professionalism

The librarian will be able to:

1. Develop and demonstrate leadership skills in identifying the unique needs of young adults and advocating for service excellence, including equitable funding and staffing levels relative to those provided for adults and children.

2. Develop and demonstrate a commitment to professionalism and ethical behavior.

3. Plan for personal and professional growth and career development.

4. Encourage young adults to become lifelong library users by helping them to discover what libraries offer, how to use library resources, and how libraries can assist them in actualizing their overall growth and development.

5. Develop and supervise formal youth participation, such as teen advisory groups, recruitment of teen volunteers, and opportunities for employment.

6. Model commitment to building assets in youth in order to develop healthy, successful young adults.

7. Implement mentoring methods to attract, develop, and train staff working with young adults.

Area II. Knowledge of Client Group

The librarian will be able to:

1. Become familiar with the developmental needs of young adults in order to provide the most appropriate resources and services.

2. Keep up-to-date with popular culture and technological advances that interest young adults.

3. Demonstrate an understanding of, and a respect for, diverse cultural, religious, and ethnic values.

4. Identify and meet the needs of patrons with special needs.

Area III. Communication, Marketing & Outreach

The librarian will be able to:

1. Form appropriate professional relationships with young adults, providing them with the assets, inputs and resiliency factors that they need to develop into caring, competent adults.

2. Develop relationships and partnerships with young adults, administrators and other youth-serving professionals in the community by establishing regular communication and by taking advantage of opportunities to meet in person.

3. Be an advocate for young adults and effectively promote the role of the library in serving young adults, demonstrating that the provision of services to this group can help young adults build assets, achieve success, and in turn, create a stronger community.

4. Design, implement, and evaluate a strategic marketing plan for promoting young adult services in the library, schools, youth-serving agencies and the community at large.

5. Demonstrate the capacity to articulate relationships between young adult services and the parent institution's core goals and mission.

6. Establish an environment in the library wherein all staff serve young adults with courtesy and respect, and all staff are encouraged to promote programs and services for young adults.

7. Identify young adult interests and groups underserved or not yet served by the library, including at-risk teens, those with disabilities, non-English speakers, etc., as well as those with special or niche interests.

8. Promote young adult library services directly to young adults through school visits, library tours, etc., and through engaging their parents, educators and other youth-serving community partners.

Area IV. Administration

The librarian will be able to:

1. Develop a strategic plan for library service with young adults based on their unique needs.

2. Design and conduct a community analysis and needs assessment.

3. Apply research findings towards the development and improvement of young adult library services.

4. Design activities to involve young adults in planning and decision-making.

5. Develop, justify, administer, and evaluate a budget for young adult services.

6. Develop physical facilities dedicated to the achievement of young adult service goals.

7. Develop written policies that mandate the rights of young adults to equitable library service.

8. Design, implement, and evaluate an ongoing program of professional development for all staff, to encourage and inspire continual excellence in service to young adults.

9. Identify and defend resources (staff, materials, facilities, funding) that will improve library service to young adults.

10. Document young adult programs and activities so as to contribute to institutional and professional memory.

11. Develop and manage services that utilize the skills, talents, and resources of young adults in the school or community.

Area V. Knowledge of Materials

The librarian will be able to:

1. Meet the informational and recreational needs of young adults through the development of an appropriate collection for all types of readers and non-readers.

2. Develop a collection development policy that supports and reflect the needs and interests of young adults and is consistent with the parent institution's mission and policies.

3. Demonstrate a knowledge and appreciation of literature for and by young adults in traditional and emerging formats.

4. Develop a collection of materials from a broad range of selection sources, and for a variety of reading skill levels, that encompasses all appropriate formats, including, but not limited to, media that reflect varied and emerging technologies, and materials in languages other than English.

5. Serve as a knowledgeable resource to schools in the community as well as parents and caregivers on materials for young adults.

Area VI. Access to Information

The librarian will be able to:

1. Organize physical and virtual collections to maximize easy, equitable, and independent access to information by young adults.

2. Utilize current merchandising and promotional techniques to attract and invite young adults to use the collection.

3. Provide access to specialized information (i.e., community resources, work by local youth, etc.).

4. Formally and informally instruct young adults in basic research skills, including how to find, evaluate, and use information effectively.

5. Be an active partner in the development and implementation of technology and electronic resources to ensure young adults' access to knowledge and information.

6. Maintain awareness of ongoing technological advances and how they can improve access to information for young adults.

Area VII. Services

The librarian will be able to:

1. Design, implement and evaluate programs and services within the framework of the library's strategic plan and based on the developmental needs of young adults and the public assets libraries represent, with young adult involvement whenever possible.

2. Identify and plan services with young adults in non-traditional settings, such as hospitals, home-school settings, alternative education, foster care programs, and detention facilities.

3. Provide a variety of informational and recreational services to meet the diverse needs and interests of young adults and to direct their own personal growth and development.

4. Continually identify trends and pop-culture interests of young people to inform, and direct their recreational collection and programming needs.

5. Instruct young adults in basic information gathering, research skills and information literacy skills - including those necessary to evaluate and use electronic information sources - to develop life-long learning habits.

6. Actively involve young adults in planning and implementing services and programs for their age group through advisory boards, task forces, and by less formal means (i.e., surveys, one-on-one discussion, focus groups, etc.)

7. Create an environment that embraces the flexible and changing nature of young adults' entertainment, technological and informational needs.

YALSA's Teen Space Guidelines

FOREWORD

These guidelines were created in 2011–2012 by a task force of the Young Adult Library Services Association (YALSA) with feedback from the library community achieved through a public comment period in the fall of 2011. Members of the task force were Katherine Trouern-Trend (chair), Audrey Sumser, Kathy Mahoney, Caroline Aversano, Samantha Marker, and Kimberly Bolan Cullin. YALSA's Board of Directors adopted the guidelines on May 24, 2012.

INTRODUCTION

This is a tool for evaluating a public library's overall level of success in providing physical and virtual space dedicated to teens, aged 12-18. Potential users of these national guidelines include library administrators, library trustees, teen services librarians, community members and job-seekers hoping to assess a library's commitment to teen services. Not every element of the guidelines may apply to every public library situation, but the guidelines can serve as a place to begin the conversation about what constitutes excellent public library space for teens.

Teens experience rapid physical, emotional and social changes while developing their intellectual capabilities and personal values, understanding and accepting their sexuality, and identifying their educational and occupational options. Libraries are vital to today's teens in order for them to achieve a successful transition from childhood to adulthood. They offer the resources and the environment that foster positive intellectual, emotional and social development of tomorrow's adults. All of these factors contribute to the need for distinct teen spaces, both in-library and virtually. The national guidelines that follow are intended for all library personnel working with and for teens, so they can fully understand the mission of library service to this frequently underserved age group and the importance of dedicated physical and virtual teen spaces for their continued engagement, growth and achievement.

The mission of the Young Adult Library Services Association (YALSA) is to expand and strengthen library services for teens. Through its member-driven advocacy, research, and professional development initiatives, YALSA builds the capacity of libraries and librarians to engage, serve, and empower teens and young adults. YALSA is a subspecialty of the American Library Association, the world's largest and oldest library organization, and a financially stable 501(c)3 not-for-profit.

To learn more about YALSA or to access other national guidelines relating to library services to teens, go to www.ala.org/yalsa.

GUIDELINES FOR PHYSICAL SPACE

1.0 Solicit teen feedback and input in the design and creation of the teen space.

A cornerstone of teen library services is the principle that teens must be actively involved in decisions regarding collections, services, and programs intended for them. Their active participation ensures that the evolving needs and interests of teens are being addressed, and they play a key role in attracting peers to the library. Teens become lifelong library users and supporters when they are enthusiastically engaged in planning and decision-making, and their sense of ownership will enhance the quality of their library experience.

1.1 Create a space that meets the needs of teens in the community by asking teens to play a role in the planning process.

1.2 Solicit teen feedback in the design of the space and regarding its use to allow teens to develop a sense of ownership.

1.3 Solicit teen feedback in the development of policies to ensure the space is representative of teen needs.

2.0 Provide a library environment that encourages emotional, social and intellectual development of teens.

Twenty-first century teens have an unprecedented power and enthusiasm in shaping their social and learning environments through the growth of digital communication. These tools have created new social norms and expectations for teens from diverse backgrounds. Public libraries must strive to recreate this online experience by hosting an inviting, high interest, multipurpose physical space for teens. In doing so, the library nurtures teens' values, identity, and the new skills necessary to grow and thrive. The environment should:

2.1 Convey that it is teen-owned and maintained.

2.2 Be comfortable, inviting, open and have a vibrant and teen-friendly look and feel.

2.3 Accommodate individual as well as group use for socializing and learning.

2.4 Include colorful and fun accessories selected by teens. Include up-to-date and teen friendly décor.

2.5 Allow for ample display of teen print, artistic and digital creations.

2.6 Allow food and drink in the space.

2.7 Contribute to a sense of teen belonging, community involvement, and library appreciation.

2.8 Be appealing to both users and non-users and provide resources for customers from diverse social groups, backgrounds and interests.

2.9 Be easy to navigate with clear signage and distinct areas for socializing, entertainment, teen print/digital collections and study and quiet areas.

2.10 Be easily navigable for teens with wheelchairs, walkers and other assistive devices

3.0. Provide a library space for teens that reflects the community in which they live.

Twenty-first century teens have the ability to select and engage in communities of their choice based on interest and identification with cultural, social and knowledge groups. A public library must provide a space for teens that builds upon the culture and size of the teen community and facilitates user-friendly engagement in the space. The space should:

3.1 Reflect the communities the library serves.

3.2 Be proportionate in size to the percentage of a community's teen population.

3.3 Incorporate creative design and signage to make it evident that the area is for teens.

3.4 Be designed and located to accommodate noise and activity away from quiet areas of the library and the children's area.

3.5 Provide easy access to research materials and staff assistance.

3.6 Provide separate rooms for programming and quiet study spaces.

3.7 Encourage visibility for unobtrusive staff supervision.

3.8 Accommodate a variety of uses including leisure reading, socializing, and individual and group activity.

3.9 Provide workspace for the teen librarian.

3.10 Have adequate and appropriate shelving for a diverse collection, displays and exhibit space.

3.11 Designed to be handicapped accessible and in compliance with the Americans with Disabilities Act (ADA).

4.0 Provide and promote materials that support the educational and leisure needs of teens.

According to Lee Rainie, director of the Pew Internet and American Life Project, the mobile revolution has changed people's sense of time, place and presence and has lead to a new media ecology . This sets a new standard for the expected immediacy and availability of desired information in all formats. Libraries have an important role in providing appropriate materials to help teens navigate, consume and create information for entertainment and lifelong skill development.

4.1 Ensure a teen collection development policy is in place that is aligned with the mission and goals of the library and the library's overall collection development policy.

4.2 House materials within the space that address the unique emotional, intellectual, and social maturity of middle and high-school age adolescents.

4.3 Maintain a teen collection that supports and addresses the interests and needs of teens in the community.

4.4 Maintain materials that are evaluated and weeded on a timely basis for condition and relevance.

4.5 Maintain a teen collection that includes a wide variety of formats, including but not limited to:

    4.5.a Print fiction and non-fiction

    4.5.b. Music, including but not limited to CD, MP3, and other emergent technologies.

    4.5.c. Video resources, including but not limited to DVD, Blu-Ray and other emergent technologies.

    4.5.d. Downloadable books.

    4.5.e. Downloading stations for in-library use.

    4.5.f. Circulating hardware, including but not limited to laptops, eReaders, MP3 players and other emergent technologies

    4.5.g. Audiobooks and other emergent technologies.

    4.5.h. Graphic novels, manga, comic books, and anime.

    4.5.i. Video games and gaming systems.

    4.5.j. Magazines, both recreational and educational.

    4.5.k. Electronic databases and other digital research materials.

     4.5.1. Print research materials.

5.0 Ensure the teen space has appropriate acceptable use and age policies to make teens feel welcome and safe.

The teen space is intended for use by customers age 12-18 years old, and its purpose is to centralize the information and recreation resources of this age group while offering teens a safe, supportive, and positive space that is uniquely their own.

    5.1 Actively seek teen input in the creation of the teen space guidelines, empowering the teens to serve as valuable resources.

    5.2 Clearly state and display guidelines once they have been discussed and determined.

    5.3 Ensure that both staff and the public are aware of the rules and expectations for using the space.

    5.3 Address common points and behaviors within the guidelines, including but not limited to:

        5.3.a Age requirement

        5.3.b. Use of appropriate language and behavior, including no fighting, no public displays of affection, and cleaning up one's mess.

    5.4 Expect teens to respect themselves and the space and convey this clearly in the guidelines.

    5.5 Consider adopting a "teen-only" policy for use of the space to create a space that is uniquely their own. A teen-only space can:

        5.5.a. Indicate to teens that the library cares about their unique developmental, recreational, educational, and social needs.

        5.5.b. Enable teens to be themselves in a teen-friendly environment.

        5.5.c. Help teens feel more at ease in the library.

        5.5.d. Help contain noise levels that may be distracting to other patrons.

5.5.e. Contribute to the safety and well-being of teens while in the library.

5.6 Limit adult use of the teen-only space to browsing materials for a period of time not to exceed 15 minutes, adult tutors who are currently working with teen students, adults accompanied by a teen, and library staff. This space can:

5.6.a. Allow teens to feel comfortable in an area where other teens are the primary occupants.

5.6.b. Enable teens to feel safe from risky, adult-initiated interactions.

6.0 Provide furniture and technology that is practical yet adaptive.

The space is designed to accommodate a variety of activities and is flexibly arranged so these activities can take place easily. Furniture, fixtures and technology should be multifunctional and flexible so that as needs and activities change the area can be adapted accordingly. The selected furniture and fixtures should be conducive to marketing library material through displays and arrangements that stimulate discovery and use. Browsing areas for materials should encourage teens to engage in the library at their own pace and comfort level.

6.1 Have shelving for materials in various formats.

6.2 Provide comfortable and durable seating and tables for teens of all sizes and abilities. Include furniture that is wheelchair accessible.

6.3 Include furniture that is easy to move around the space in order to allow for a multitude of group, individual, and programmatic activities.

6.4 Include display equipment such as bulletin boards and display cases.

6.5 Ensure ample trash receptacles are available.

6.6 Provide a reference or information services desk or kiosk, clock, and telephone as well as ample storage for teen librarian's supplies.

6.7 Offer listening, viewing, and downloading equipment for a full range of user abilities/needs. Ensure assistive hardware and software technology is available for vision and hearing disabled teens.

6.8 Be technology rich and include both stationary and portable technology that is easily accessible and exposes teens to a diversity of hardware and software for both entertainment and learning.

6.9 Offer access to current and emerging platforms and tools, including but not limited to social-networking and photo-sharing sites, user-driven communication tools for tagging and review sharing, audio and visual production technologies, and interactive Web services.

6.10 Provide adequate lighting, ventilation, temperature controls, and acoustics.

6.11 Include ample outlets to allow for technology owned by the library as well as technology owned and brought into the space by teens.

6.12 Provide adequate network infrastructure.

6.13 Ensure wireless capability.

GUIDELINES FOR VIRTUAL SPACE

7.0 Ensure content, access and use is flexible and adaptive

Online communication and engagement is central to the rhythms of teenagers' lives. Many teens have self-structured identities and social environments online and exist in a rapidly converging virtual and physical world. According to Pew researchers, three-fourths of teenagers contribute content online and are key players in the digital information revolution. Traditionally libraries have sought to push information out to library users through librarian-created content, but it is vital in today's world to recognize and adapt to the changing information needs and expectations of our teen patrons. Teens should be active participants in the creation and maintenance of the library's online presence. An attractive and functional virtual space should be designed with teen input, evaluated regularly by teens, have interactive features, and be usable on a mobile device. The virtual space should:

7.1 Support and use social media as a vital means of communication.

7.2 Allow teens to share their work, receive feedback and build community.

7.3 Model safe and appropriate use of social media tools for teens.

7.4 Support collaboration with adults and peers.

7.5 Allow administrative rights and content contribution to both library staff and teens.

7.6 Be interactive.

7.7 Support and feature mechanisms for teens to connect in real time virtually with library staff who can assist them with research needs such as chat, text message, and Skype, among others.

7.8 Support and feature mechanisms for teens to connect with one another through the library website to talk about books, homework, and research.

7.9 Support and provide capabilities for taking part in programs virtually.

7.10 Offer classes, drop-in sessions, and/or virtual instruction to educate and teach use of Web 2.0 tools and other emerging technologies.

7.11 Provide positive online interactions modeled by library staff.

7.12 Include content, photos and videos produced by teens in accordance with the library's photo release policy.

7.13 Designed to be accessible for those with visual, auditory, and motor disabilities. See The Internet and Web-based Content Accessibility Checklist (http://www.ala.org/ascla/ asclaprotools/thinkaccessible/internetwebguidelines) provided by the Association for Specialized and Cooperative Library Agencies.

8.0 Ensure the virtual space reflects 21st century learning standards.

Through interaction and participation in digital media, teens are developing important social and technical skills helping to build a skill set necessary to learn and thrive in today's networked world. As virtual and physical worlds continue to converge, teens need tools, support and resources to harness information in a way that is meaningful to their particular needs and as participants in multiple and diverse social and learning environments.

8.1 Help teens thrive in a complex information environment.

8.2 Expose teens to diverse perspectives, gather and use information ethically and use social tools responsibly and safely.

8.3 Support the development of multiple literacies including digital, visual, textual and technological information navigation and use.

8.4 Enhance teen information literacy skills through opportunities to share and learn with others, both physically and virtually.

8.5 Teach respect for copyright and the intellectual property rights of creators and producers.

8.6 Connect understanding to the real world.

8.7 Help teens consider diverse and global perspectives.

8.8 Engage teens in social and intellectual networks of learning to gather and share information.

8.9 Use technology and other information tools to organize and display knowledge and understanding in ways that others can view, use, and assess.

8.10 Help teens connect learning to community issues.

8.11 Contribute to the exchange of ideas within and beyond the learning community.

8.12 Respect the principles of intellectual freedom.

8.13 Use creative and artistic formats to express personal learning.

9.0 Provide digital resources for teens that meet their unique and specific needs.

21st century teens interact with a range of materials in multiple formats in their school and leisure environments. According to the MacArthur Foundation, we are in the midst of a knowledge revolution that is changing how we approach learning and leisure resources for youth. Libraries need to adapt to this new paradigm and provide resources and support for teen's natural gravitation to digital media platforms.

9.1 Provide general contact information for the library and specific contact information for the teen librarian and teen content creators.

9.2 Feature information about library programs and activities for teens.

9.3 Feature a collection development policy for website content and links that includes a procedure for addressing challenges to controversial websites and a procedure for users to suggest additional electronic resources.

9.4 Feature annotated booklists and book reviews, and/or links to teen literature sites that provide reader's advisory services.

9.5 Promote teen collections and resources.

9.6 Feature informational and recreational links, including the library catalog, databases, and recreational links suggested by teens.

9.7 Feature interactive information of interest and need to teens including, but not limited to, homework help; health and sexuality; financial advice; relationship advice; time management tips; pop culture; college prep.

9.8 Provide opportunities for teens to post reviews of materials.

9.9 Provide links to the library's Teen Advisory Board blog, wiki, Twitter feed, or other means of online communication.

9.10 Feature interactive content that helps teens learn how to use library resources.

9.11 Feature content that is changed and updated frequently.

REVIEW PROCESS

In order to finalize the Guidelines, the Taskforce presented a draft document to YALSA'S Board of Directors in June 2011. At this meeting, the Taskforce solicited feedback on the draft

The feedback was carefully considered by the Taskforce; additions and revisions have been made accordingly. This draft document was approved for dissemination via a call for public comments period on Oct. 14, 2011. After the public comment period closed, the Taskforce reviewed the feedback received and refined the draft guidelines as appropriate. The goal is to have the guidelines finalized by January 2012. The Public Library Guidelines Taskforce wishes to thank the library community for their contributions to this document. It is intended that the Guidelines for Services to Teens will be reviewed for revisions every five years.

RESOURCES

American Association of School Librarians. 2007. "Standards for the 21st Century Learner." Accessed May 31, 2012. www.ala .org/aasl/sites/ala.org.aasl/files/content/guidelinesandstandards/ learningstandards/AASL_LearningStandards.pdf.

Apple in Education. "Useful to Everyone, Right from the Start." Accessed May 31, 2012. www.apple.com/education/special-education/

Association of Specialized and Cooperative Library Agencies. 2010. "Assistive Technology: What You Need to Know." www .ala.org/ascla/sites/ala.org.ascla/files/content/asclaprotools/ accessibilitytipsheets/tipsheets/11-Assistive_Technol.pdf

Bernier, Anthony. 2010. "Spacing Out with Young Adults: Translating YA Space Concepts Back into Practice." In The Information Needs and Behaviors of Urban Teens: Research and Practice, edited by Denise E. Agosto and Sandra Hughes-Hassell, 113-126. Chicago: ALA Editions.

Bernier, Anthony. 2010. "Ten Years of 'YA Spaces of Your Dreams': What Have We Learned?" Voice of Youth Advocates Online. Accessed May 31, 2012. www.voya.com/2010/05/13/ten-years-of-ya-spaces-of-your-dreams-what-have-we-learned.

Bernier, Anthony. 2009. "'A Space for Myself to Go': Early Patterns in Small YA Spaces." Public Libraries 48(5): 33–47.

Bernier, Anthony and Nicole Branch. 2009. "A TeenZone: Humming Its Own New Tune." Voice of Youth Advocates 32(3): 204–206.

Bernier, Anthony, ed. 2012. YA Spaces of Your Dreams Collection. Bowie, Md.: VOYA Press.

Bolan, Kimberly. 2011. "Best Practice in Teen Space Design Webinar. Accessed May 31, 2012. www.ala.org/yalsa/onlinelearning/webinars/webinarsondemand

Bolan, Kimberly. 2008. "YALSA White Paper: The Need for Teen Spaces in Public Libraries." Accessed May 31, 2012. www.ala.org/yalsa/guidelines/whitepapers/teenspaces.

Bolan (Taney), Kimberly. 2008. Teen Spaces: The Step-by-Step Library Makeover. Chicago: ALA Editions.

Braun, Linda. 2010. "The Big App : New York Libraries Take Homework Help Mobile — with a Little Help from Their Friends." School Library Journal. Accessed May 31, 2012. www.schoollibraryjournal.com/slj/home/887747-312/the_big_app_new_yorks.html.csp.

Braun, Linda. 2006. "Instant Messages." YALSABlog. Accessed May 31, 2012. http://yalsa.ala.org/blog/2006/03/12/instant-messages.

Braun, Linda. 2010. "Whose Space Is It?" YALSABlog, Accessed May 31, 2012. http://yalsa.ala.org/blog/2010/03/05/whose-space-is-it/

Daly, Erin. 2012. "30 Days of Innovation: Incorporate Art Into Your Teen Space." YALSABlog, Accessed May 31, 2012. http://yalsa.ala.org/blog/2012/04/11/30-days-of-innovation-11-incorporate-teen-art-into-your-space/

Duffy, Mairead. 2012. "30 Days of Innovation #5: Changing Your Point of Reference." YALSABlog. Accessed May 31, 2012. http://yalsa.ala.org/blog/2012/04/05/30-days-of-innovation-5-changing-your-point-of-reference/

Farrelly, Michael Garrett. 2012. Make Room for Teens: A Guide to Developing Teen Spaces in Libraries. Santa Barbara, Calif.: Libraries Unlimited.

Feinberg, Sandra and James R Keller. 2010. Designing Space for Children and Teens in Public Spaces and Libraries. Chicago: ALA Editions.

Fialkoff, Francine. 2010. "Third Place or Thinking Space." Library Journal. Accessed on May 31, 2012. www.libraryjournal.com/article/CA6716262.html

Flowers, Sarah. 2010. Young Adults Deserve the Best: YALSA's Competencies in Action. Chicago : ALA Editions, 2010.

Ito, Mizuko, et. al. 2009. Hanging Out, Messing Around, and Geeking Out: Kids Living and Learning with New Media. Cambridge, Mass.: MIT Press, 2009.

Ito, Mizuko, et al. 2008. "Living and Learning with New Media : Summary of Findings from the Digital Youth Project. Accessed May 31, 2012. http://digitalyouth.ischool.berkeley.edu/files/report/digitalyouth-WhitePaper.pdf.

Jones, Patrick, Mary K. Chelton and Joel Shoemaker. 2001. Do It Right: Best Practices for Serving Teens in School and Public Libraries. New York: Neal-Schuman.

King, David Lee. 2011. "Content Creation, Media Labs, and Hackerspaces." David Lee King Blog. Accessed May 31, 2012. www.davidleeking.com/2011/12/15/content-creation-media-labs-and-hackerspaces/#.T8IwbZlYt2k.

Lenhart, Amanda, et al. 2011. "Teen Kindness and Cruelty on Social Network Sites." Pew Internet and American Life Project. Accessed May 31, 2012. http://pewinternet.org/Reports/2011/Teens-and-social-media.aspx.

Library Journal and School Library Journal. The Digital Shift: Libraries and New Media. Accessed May 31, 2012. www.thedigitalshift.com.

Library Roadshow. 2012. "Michelle Shows Us ImaginOn's Teen Space." Video. Accessed May 31, 2012. http://youtu.be/5cubsGMSlnA.

McGrath, Renee. 2011. "Creating a Mobile Booklist 'App.'" Young Adult Library Services 10 (2): 35–37.

McCue, T.J. 2011. "First Public Library To Create a Maker Space." Forbes. Accessed May 31, 2012. www.forbes.com/sites/tjmccue/2011/11/15/first-public-library-to-create-a-maker-space/

Microsoft. "Microsoft Accessibility: Technology for Everyone." Accessed May 31, 2012. www.microsoft.com/enable.

KQED. Mind/Shift: How We Will Learn. Accessed May 31, 2012. http://blogs.kqed.org/mindshift.

Peoski, Laura. "Where Are All the Teens? Engaging and Empowering them Online." Young Adult Library Services 8(2): 26–28.

Rainie, Lee and Susannah Fox. 2012. "Just in Time Information through Mobile Connections." Pew Internet and American Life Project. Accessed May 31, 2012. www.pewinternet.org/Reports/2012/Just-in-time.aspx.

Rainie, Lee. 2011. "Libraries and the New Community Information Ecology." Video presentation. Accessed May 31, 2012. www.pewinternet.org/Presentations/2011/Apr/Beyond-Books.aspx.

Reeder, Jessica. 2011. "Are Maker Spaces the Future of Libraries." Shareable: Science & Tech. Accessed May 31, 2012. www.shareable.net/blog/the-future-of-public-libraries-maker-spaces.

Search Institute. "Developmental Assets Lists." Accessed May 31, 2012. www.search-institute.org/developmental-assets/lists.

Toppo, Greg. 2010. "Digital LibraryAims to Expand Kids' Media Literacy." USA Today. Accessed May 31, 2012. www.usatoday.com/news/education/story/2011-10-09/chicago-teens-build-media-literacy-in-digital-library/50714312/1.

Watters, Audrey. 2011. "Libraries and Museums Become Hands-On Learning Labs." KQED Mind/Shift. Accessed May 31, 2012. http://blogs.kqed.org/mindshift/2011/11/libraries-and-museums-set-to-become-hands-on-learning-labs.

YOUmedia. YOUMedia Web site. Accessed May 31, 2012. www.youmedia.org.

Ypulse. 2010. "Ypulse Interview: Kim Bolan Cullin: 'Teen Spaces.'" Accessed May 31, 2012. www.ypulse.com/post/view/ypulse-interview-kim-bolan-cullin-teen-spaces

A SELECTION OF MODEL PHYSICAL AND VIRTUAL TEEN SPACES (AS OF APRIL 2012)

Library:	Frankfort Community Public Library
Location:	Frankfort, IN
Teen Space Name:	The Edge
Link:	http://fcpl.accs.net/teen.htm
Contact Information:	Tom Smith, Assistant Director and Kirsten Weaver, Teen and Outreach Librarian

Library:	Waupaca Area Public Library
Location:	Waupaca, WI
Teen Space Name:	Best Cellar
Link:	www.waupacalibrary.org/teens
Contact Information:	Peg Burington, Director

Library:	Newark Public Library
Location:	Newark, NY
Teen Space Name:	The Teen Spot
Link:	http://newarklibraryteenspot.blogspot.com/
Contact Information:	Elly Dawson, Director

Library:	Plymouth District Library
Location:	Plymouth, MI
Teen Space Name:	Teen Zone
Link:	http://plymouthlibrary.org/index.php/teen
Contact Information:	Cathy Lichtman, Teen Service Librarian

Library:	Farmington Public Library
Location:	Farmington, New Mexico
Teen Space Name:	Teen Zone
Link:	www.infoway.org/TeenZone/index.asp
Contact Information:	Barbara Savage Huff, Youth Services Librarian

Library:	Chicago Public Libary, Harold Washington Library Center
Location:	Chicago, IL
Teen Space Name:	YouMedia
Link:	http://youmediachicago.org/2-about-us/pages/2-about-us
Contact Information:	Mike Hawkins, YouMedia Coordinator/Lead Mentor

Library:	Tacoma Public Library
Location:	Tacoma, WA
Teen Space Name:	Story Lab
Link:	www.storylabtacoma.org/
Contact Information:	Sara Sunshine Holloway, Librarian

Library:	Queens Library
Location #1:	Queens Library for Teens, Far Rockaway, NY
Link:	www.facebook.com/queenslibraryforteens
Location #2:	Flushing Branch, Flushing, NY http://queenslibrary.org/index.aspx?page_id=44&branch_id=F
Contact Information:	Vikki Terrile, Coordinator of Young Adult Services

Library:	Detroit Public Library
Location:	Detroit, MI
Teen Space Name:	H.Y.P.E. (Helping Young People Excel)
Link:	http://dplhype.org/
Contact Information:	Lurine Carter, Children's and Youth Services Coordinator

Library:	Orange County Library System
Location:	Orlando, FL
Teen Space Name:	Club Central
Link:	www.ocls.info/Children/Teen/doit/club_central_do_it.asp

Contact Information:	Vera Gubnitskaia, Youth Services Manager
Library:	Gail Borden Public Library District
Location:	Elgin, IL
Teen Space Name:	Studio 270
Link:	www.gailborden.info/m/content/view/1302/905/
Contact Information:	Billie Jo Moffett and Melissa Lane, Studio 270 Co-Managers

YALSA White Papers

White Paper No. 1
Why Teen Space?
Kimberly Bolan, MLS, Library Consultant
Accepted by the YALSA Board of Directors, June 2007

This paper provides an overview of and commentary on teen space development and its implicit bearing on the strategic vision, planning, and development of facilities design for twenty-first-century libraries. Attention will be drawn to key success factors such as why teen space is important and current and future priorities and best practices related to library facilities for teenage users. This paper will help you understand the importance of teen space within your community and organization, and address issues that shape the quality of a teen customer's experience with your library.

BACKGROUND

Over the past twelve years, there has been a transformation in library facility design for teens. Traditionally speaking, common practice has been to ignore dedicated space for teens or to create boring, unfriendly facilities with little attention to adolescent needs and wants. Libraries have generally been designed without teen customers in mind, driven by librarian, administrator, and architect personal likes and ideas. Today more and more schools and public libraries are working to accommodate 13- to 18-year-olds, moving away from the previously described "traditional" approaches to creating more efficient, innovative, appealing, and teen-inspired spaces.

POSITION

As libraries continue to move forward, organizations of all types, sizes, and budgets must realize that warm, inviting, comfortable, and user-centered environments are integral in attracting teenage users and transforming the role and image of the library. Such environments are essential in encouraging positive use of libraries for recreational activities, learning, and education.

Whether building a new library, renovating an existing facility, or working on a minor facilities revamp, the primary key success factor is understanding why teen space is critical. Developing dedicated, attractive, motivating, and teen-oriented space provides a way to

- create a positive, safe environment for studying, socializing, and leisure activities
- outwardly and interactively acknowledge teen customers and their needs by supporting adolescent asset development; creating an environment that encourages emotional, social, and intellectual development; and building a sense of teen belonging, community involvement, and library appreciation
- expand your customer base by appealing to users and non-users, creating a wider variety of customers from a diverse social groups, backgrounds, and interests
- effectively market library services by drawing teens into the physical library space, leading them to other library services such as materials, programming, etc.
- increase current and future library supporters: the future of libraries is tomorrow's adults and, believe it or not, these are today's teens

Other key success teen space factors include the following:

- Making teen participation and input a priority as well as a regular practice throughout the planning, design, implementation, maintenance, and marketing of the space and related teen library services.
- Appropriately sizing a teen facility based on a library's community/student population (ages 13–18). Libraries must reevaluate space allocations in their overall facilities and scale them according to demographics, not personal bias. In public library facilities, the ratio of a teen area to the overall library should be equal to the ratio of the teen population of that community to the overall population of that community.
- Developing a well-thought-out plan for improvement, including short-term and long-range planning for current and future teen space and services.
- Getting buy-in and support from all stakeholders, including teens, staff, faculty, administrators, and the community.
- Creating a truly teen-friendly space that is comfortable, colorful, interactive, flexible in design, and filled with technology. It is important to keep in mind that "teen-friendly" is not synonymous with unruly, unreasonable, impractical, or tacky.
- Thinking about what teens *need*, not about what adults *want*. Don't make assumptions or let personal biases impact decision making, whether selecting furniture, shelving/displays, flooring, lighting, paint color, signage, etc. Items should be welcoming, have visual impact, be versatile, and encourage positive, independent use of the facility.

CONCLUSION

Making libraries appealing and important to teens is not an impossible task. Library facilities design is one integral step in attracting teen customers and redefining libraries of the future. Looking at teen facilities design in a new light, letting go of antiquated ideas, reevaluating traditional ways of "doing business," and emphasizing customer needs and wants are essential first steps in moving forward in the world of twenty-first-century libraries.

REFERENCES

Bernier, A., ed.. *Making Space for Teens: Recognizing Young Adult Needs in Library Buildings*. Scarecrow Press, forthcoming.

Bolan, Kimberly. **"Looks Like Teen Spirit."** *School Library Journal* 52, no. 1 (November 2006): 44+.

Bolan, Kimberly. *Teen Spaces: The Step-by-Step Library Makeover*. 2nd ed. ALA Editions, 2009.

Jones, Patrick, Mary Kay Chelton, and Joel Shoemaker. *Do It Right: Best Practices for Serving Young Adults in School and Public Libraries*. Neal-Schuman, 2001.

Search Institute. "The 40 Developmental Assets for Adolescents (Ages 12–18)" (2007).www.search-institute.org/content/40-developmental-assets-adolescents-ages-12-18. Retrieved June 14, 2007.

White Paper No. 2
The Value of Young Adult Literature
Michael Cart

To ask "What is the value of young adult literature?" is to beg at least three other questions:

1. What is meant by "value"?
2. What is meant by "young adult"?
3. What is meant by "literature"?

To answer these questions, in turn

1. "Value" is defined, simply, as "worth." When used in juxtaposition with the term "young adult literature," it invites an assessment of how worthwhile, important, or desirable that literature is—measured, as we will see below, in terms both of its aesthetic success and its personal impact on readers and their lives.

2. "Young Adult" is officially defined by YALSA as meaning persons twelve to eighteen years of age. Unofficially, however, it is acknowledged that "young adult" is an amorphous term that is subject to continuous revision as demanded by changing societal views. Since the early 1990s, for example, it has (again, unofficially) been expanded to include those as young as ten and, since the late 1990s, as old as twenty-five (or even, some would argue, thirty).

3. "Literature" has traditionally meant published prose—both fiction and nonfiction—and poetry. The increasing importance of visual communication has begun to expand this definition to include the pictorial, as well, especially when offered in combination with text as in the case of picture books, comics, and graphic novels and nonfiction.

Often the word "literature" is also presumed to imply aesthetic merit. However, because young adults have, historically, been accorded such scant respect by society—being viewed more as homogeneous problems than as individual persons—the literature that has been produced for them has, likewise, been dismissed as little more than problem-driven literature of problematic value. Accordingly, the phrase "young adult literature" has itself been dismissed as being an oxymoron.

The Young Adult Library Services Association takes strenuous exception to all of this. Founded in a tradition of respect for those it defines as "young adults," YALSA respects young adult literature as well. A proof of this is the establishment of the Michael L. Printz Award, which YALSA presents annually to the author of the best young adult book of the year, "best" being defined solely in terms of literary merit. In this way, YALSA values young adult literature—*as literature*—for its artistry and its aesthetic integrity.

But to invoke the Printz Award is to invite one last definition: this time of the very phrase "young adult literature," for—like "young adult"—this is an inherently amorphous and dynamic descriptor. Narrowly defined, it means literature specifically published *for* young adults. More broadly, however, it can mean anything that young adults read, though it must—of necessity—have a young adult protagonist and addressing issues of interest to this readership. This broader definition is demonstrated by YALSA's annual selection of what it calls "Best Books for Young Adults," a list that often includes books published for adults and even, sometimes, for children.

Whether young adult literature is defined narrowly or broadly, however, much of its value is to be found in how it addresses the needs of its readers. Often described as "developmental," these books acknowledge that young adults are beings in evolution, in search of self and identity; beings who are constantly growing and changing, morphing from the condition of childhood to that of adulthood. That period of passage called "young adulthood" is a unique part of life, distinguished by unique needs that are—at minimum—physical, intellectual, emotional, and societal in nature. By addressing these needs, young adult literature is made valuable not only by its artistry but also by its relevance to the lives of its readers. And by addressing not only their needs but also their interests, the literature becomes a powerful inducement for them to read, another compelling reason to value it.

Yet another of the chief values of young adult literature is to be found in its capacity to offer readers an opportunity to see themselves reflected in its pages. Young adulthood is, intrinsically, a period of tension. On the one hand, young adults have an all-consuming need to belong. But on the other, they are also inherently solipsistic, regarding themselves as being unique, which is not cause for celebration but, rather, for despair. For to be unique is to be unlike one's peers, to be "other," in fact. And to be "other" is to not belong but, instead, to be an outcast. Thus, to see oneself in the pages of a young adult book is to receive the blessed reassurance that one is not alone after all, not other, not alien but, instead, a viable part of a larger community of beings who share a common humanity.

Another value of young adult literature is its capacity to foster understanding, empathy, and compassion by offering vividly realized portraits of the lives—exterior and interior—of individuals who are *un*like the reader. In this way, young adult literature invites its readership to embrace the humanity it shares with those who—if not for the encounter in reading—might forever remain strangers or—worse—irredeemably "other."

Still another value of young adult literature is its capacity for telling its readers the truth, however disagreeable that may sometimes be; for in this way, it equips readers for dealing with the realities of impending adulthood and—though it may sound quaintly old-fashioned—for assuming the rights and responsibilities of citizenship.

By giving readers such a frame of reference, it also helps them to find role models, to make sense of the world they inhabit, to develop a personal philosophy of being, to determine what is right and, equally, what is wrong, and to cultivate a personal sensibility. To, in other words, become civilized.

So what, finally, is the value of young adult literature? One might as well ask, "What is the value of breathing?"—for both are essential, even fundamental, to life and survival.

White Paper No. 3

The Benefits of Including Dedicated Young Adult Librarians
on Staff in the Public Library

YALSA with Audra Caplan

BACKGROUND

The Young Adult Library Services Association adopted a strategic plan in 2004. That plan included a Core Purpose and a Vivid Description of the Desired Future. The Core Purpose is "to advocate for excellence in library services to the teen population." The first bullet below the description states: "There will be a young adult librarian in every public and secondary school library." The group of practitioners who developed both of these statements understood that advocating excellence in library service for teens goes hand in hand with the provision of a dedicated young adult librarian in each location that serves teens.

POSITION

Why is it important to have young adult librarians on staff?

Because a significant percent of the American population is composed of adolescents and many of them are library users. There are over 30 million teens currently in the United States, the largest generation since the baby boomers, and, according to a 2007 survey of young people conducted by a Harris Poll for the Young Adult Library Services Association (YALSA 2004), 78% of these teen respondents have library cards. Not surprisingly, participation in library programs by youth under age 18 has been rising steadily over the past decade, from 35.5 million per year in 1993 to more than 51.8 million in 2001 (Americans for Libraries Council 2006). We also know that while 14.3 million kindergarteners through 12th graders are home alone after school every day (Afterschool Alliance 2006), three-quarters of Americans believe it is a high priority for public libraries to offer a safe place where teens can study and congregate (Public Agenda 2006).

Unfortunately, many communities do not provide after school or weekend activities that can engage teens, despite the understanding that successful, well-prepared young adults are essential to fill roles as contributing members of a vital society, and that teens need responsive and responsible venues in which to develop into successful, contributing members of society.

Why can't generalist library staff serve the teen population as well as young adult librarians?

Because librarians especially trained to work with young adults are age-level specialists who understand that teens have unique needs and have been trained especially to work with this particular population. As books like Barbara Strauch's *The Primal Teen: What New Discoveries about the Teenage Brain Tell Us about Our Kids* have shown us, teens' brains and bodies are different from a child's or an adult's. As a result, their behavior, interests, and informational and social needs are not the same as those of children or adults.

The Chapin Hall Center for Children, www.chapinhall.org, completed a study in 2004 on "Teens in the Library." In the area of staffing, the first statement related to Improving youth services in libraries is that "dedicated staff are essential to effective youth programs." Across all of the sites studied by Chapin Hall and the Urban Institute, senior administrators and librarians agreed that "youth programs require a staff person whose priority is to manage the program. . . ." Library services that best address teen needs and interests are the professional priority of young adult librarians.

Why provide staff and services specifically for teens?

Dedicated library services for teens improves the library as a whole. Armed with knowledge and understanding of adolescent behavior, interests, and needs, young adult librarians create programming and build collections appropriate to the concerns of young adults and develop services based on knowledge of adolescent development. They are experts in the field of young adult literature and keep up with current teen trends in reading, technology, education, and popular culture. They provide reference services that help young adults find and use information, and they promote activities that build and strengthen information literacy skills. They know the benefits of youth participation and understand it is essential to the offer of excellent service to teens, encouraging teens to provide direct input to library service through activities such as teen advisory groups and volunteer or paid work in libraries. They also collaborate with other youth development experts in the community and with agencies that provide services to teens.

According to key findings from the Wallace Foundation's "Public Libraries as Partners in Youth Development (PLPYD)," public libraries selected for this program were challenged to "develop or expand youth programs that engaged individual teens in a developmentally supportive manner while enhancing library services for all youth in the community." Based on the experiences of the PLPYD sites, the findings conclude that "Public Libraries have the potential to design youth programs that provide developmentally enriching experiences to teens and have positive effect both on youth services and the library more broadly."

Young adult librarians build relationships with teens and help other staff to feel comfortable with them. One of the findings from a study by Chapin Hall indicated that staff prejudice in relation to teens broke down when staff can be mentored to develop relationships with teens. Youth development principles were credited with changing the general culture of the library by providing an "important new language" for library administrators that helped the library to establish a new leadership role in the area of youth development and in the community. In an era when libraries must clearly articulate their importance to the larger community, the role of youth development agency increases the public library's value as an institution and also makes good economic sense for the community.

A 2007 survey conducted by the Harris Poll for YALSA asked young people what needed to happen in their local library in order for them to use it more often. One in five respondents said they would use their library more if "there was a librarian just for teens." One-third of respondents said that they would use the library more if the library had more interesting materials to borrow and events to attend.

The young adult librarian acts as a significant adult in the lives of many young people, thereby meeting one of the seven developmental needs of teens: positive social interaction with peers and adults (Search Institute).

CONCLUSION

Why employ young adult librarians?

The practical reasons are listed above. On a fundamental level, the goal is to provide excellent service to a large but unique segment of the population, teens. Young adult librarians are essential to providing the best service to young adults in libraries, and they are essential to keeping libraries viable and up-to-date by translating knowledge about cultural trends into programs, collections, staff engagement with youth, and collaborative efforts in the broader community. So the answer is simple—employing young adult librarians is the smart thing to do.

REFERENCES

Afterschool Alliance. 2006, November 13. "7 in 10 Voters Want New Congress to Increase Funding for Afterschool Programs, Poll Finds." Press release.

Americans for Libraries Council. 2006. "Learning in Motion: A Sampling of Library Teen Programs." www.publicagenda.org/files/research_facts/long_overdue_teens_fact_sheet.pdf. Accessed December 28, 2007.

Chapin Hall Center for Children. 2005. "New on the Shelf: Teens in the Library." www.chapinhall.org/research/report/new-shelf. Accessed September 27, 2008.

Harris Interactive, Inc. 2007. "Youth and Library Use Study." www.ala.org/ala/mgrps/divs/yalsa/HarrisYouthPoll.pdf. American Library Association.

Jones, Patrick. 2003. *New Directions for Library Service to Young Adults.* ALA Editions/Young Adult Library Services Association.

Public Agenda. 3006. "Long Overdue: A Fresh Look at Public and Leadership Attitudes about Libraries in the 21st Century." www.publicagenda.org/files/pdf/Long_Overdue.pdf. Accessed December 28, 2007.

Public Library Association. 2007. *2007 PLDS Statistical Report.* PLA.

Spillett, Roxanne. 2002, October 3. "When School Day Ends, Danger Begins for the Young." *Atlanta Journal-Constitution.*

Strauch, Barbara. 2003. *The Primal Teen: What New Discoveries about the Teenage Brain Tell Us about Our Kids.* Doubleday.

Wallace Foundation. N.d. "Public Libraries as Partners in Youth Development (PLPYD)." www.wallacefoundation. org/GrantsPrograms/FocusAreasPrograms/Libraries/Pages/ PublicLibrariesasPartnersinYouthDevelopment.aspx.

YALSA. 2004. "Competencies for Librarians Serving Youth: Young Adults Deserve the Best."www.ala.org/ala/mgrps/divs/yalsa/profdev/ youngadultsdeserve.cfm.

White Paper No. 4
The Importance of Young Adult Services in LIS Curricula
Don Latham, on behalf of the Young Adult Library Services Association

ABSTRACT

This white paper discusses the importance of educational programs for training young adult librarians within schools of library and information science (LIS). It describes the evolution of library services to young adults as well as education for young adult librarians. It identifies the various competencies needed by young adult librarians in the twenty-first century and situates these competencies within the larger context of LIS curricula. Finally, it concludes by emphasizing the value of young adult library services courses both for professionals-in-training and for young adults.

BACKGROUND

American libraries have a long and proud tradition of providing services to young adults (defined by the Young Adult Library Services Association as young people ages 12 to 18). The Brooklyn Youth Library opened in Brooklyn, New York, in 1823, nearly 75 years before psychologist G. Stanley Hall introduced the concept of "adolescence" into the popular parlance (Bernier et al. 2005). In the twentieth century, the profession saw a burgeoning in young adult services in libraries, particularly in the period following World War II. As a result, in 1957 the American Library Association established the Young Adult Services Division (now the Young Adult Library Services Association) as a separate entity from the Children's Library Association (Bernier et al. 2005). Over the years, the profession has produced a number of outstanding librarians and advocates for young adult services, among them Margaret Edwards, the young people's librarian at Enoch Pratt Free Library in Baltimore (Bernier et al. 2005), and Michael Printz, a school librarian in Topeka, Kansas (YALSA n.d.), both of whom now have young adult book awards named for them.

Concomitant with this growth in library services for young adults has been a growth in programs for educating young adult librarians. Some of the earliest of these included the Pratt Institute in Brooklyn, Case

Western in Cleveland, and the Carnegie Library of Pittsburgh's Training School for Children's Librarians (Jenkins 2000). Now most schools of library and information science offer at least one course in young adult resources and/or services, and many offer multiple courses. A search of the Association for Library and Information Science Education (ALISE) membership directory reveals that approximately 13% of ALISE members identify "young adult services" as one of their teaching and/or research areas (ALISE 2007).

And, indeed, the need for young adult services in libraries is greater than ever before. According to the U.S. Census, the number of young people ages 10 to 19 increased from approximately 35 million in 1990 to over 40 million in 2000 and to nearly 42 million by 2007 (U.S. Census Bureau 2008). In addition to the increasing numbers of young adults, there has been an explosion in information technologies, a proliferation of resource formats (and user preferences), and a growing emphasis on the importance of information literacy (Jones et al. 2004), all of which have presented both exciting opportunities and formidable challenges for librarians who serve young adults.

POSITION

The Young Adult Library Services Association (YALSA) is committed to the philosophy that "young adults deserve the best." Recognizing the varied knowledge and skill sets needed to provide exemplary services to young adults in the twenty-first century, the division works to promote a rich and diverse educational experience for students preparing to become young adult librarians as well as other information professionals who will work, at least in part, with young adults.

Toward that end, in 2003 the division adopted a set of core competencies for young adult librarians, in which seven areas of competency are identified: Leadership and Professionalism, Knowledge of Client Group, Communication, Administration, Knowledge of Materials, Access to Information, and Services (YALSA 2003). LIS schools can foster these competencies through various means: by offering courses devoted specifically to young adult resources, services, and programming; by incorporating discussion of young adult users and their information needs into other courses, such as reference services, media production, research methods, and information policy; and by encouraging students to gain valuable experiences outside of the classroom, through such things as internships in young adult services and membership in professional associations like YALSA and the American Association of School Librarians (AASL).

The most important competency, because it is that from which the other competencies follow, is knowledge of young adults, and LIS curricula should incorporate that topic into various courses. Knowledge of young adults includes understanding the developmental needs of teens and recognizing that these needs can be different for different teens. It also includes an understanding of the diversity among teens and an appreciation of the information needs of teens from various cultural and ethnic backgrounds. And it involves a recognition of the special needs of "extreme teens," that is, those teens who do not fit the mold of the "typical teen" perhaps because of their educational situation, their living situation, and/ or their sexuality (Anderson 2005). Knowledge of young adult users and their information needs is complemented by an understanding of how to conduct user needs assessment, so research methods should be an integral part of education for young adult librarianship.

LIS curricula should also provide education in the myriad resources that are available to today's young adults. Libraries traditionally have promoted reading, and that is still a core mission. But it is also the case that teens now engage with various forms of media in addition to print: movies, television, games (especially computer games), music, and, of course, the Internet. Young adult librarians should be conversant with the seemingly infinite variety of materials now available in order to meet the needs and preferences of the clients they serve.

Today's young adults are not only consumers of media, but also producers. Most are avid computer users, engaging in social networking, creating their own digital videos, participating in gaming, texting, instant messaging—and often doing several of these things at once! Young adult librarians certainly should be trained in the use of information technology to create and deliver information services, but they should also be educated to understand the broader cultural implications of how and why teens use technology and how this is changing the way teens interact with and process information.

Closely related to the use of technology as a way of accessing and interacting with information is the concept of information literacy. Young adult librarians should be educated to understand what information literacy is and how to promote information literacy skill development among teens. Information literacy—which may be defined as the ability to access, evaluate, and use information ethically and effectively—has received much attention both in the K–12 and higher education environments in the twenty-first century (see, for example, the standards developed by the American Association of School Librarians 1998 and the Association of College and Research Libraries 2000). Such skills are seen as increasingly necessary for success in school, the workplace, and life. The teenage years are a crucial time in the acquisition of the numerous complex skills related to information literacy, and young adult librarians can play an important role in ensuring that teens are successful in developing these abilities.

Designing effective programs to promote resources, technology, and information literacy among teens provides a way to bring together these three pillars of young adult services. LIS schools should offer courses in various types of programming as well as the marketing of services to teens. After all, today's teenaged library users will become tomorrow's adult library users—and, hopefully, library supporters. Some will even become tomorrow's librarians.

CONCLUSION

For these reasons, the Young Adult Library Services Association affirms the value and importance of young adult services in LIS curricula. Educating young adult librarians for the twenty-first century represents a commitment to helping young adults become lifelong readers, lifelong learners, and lifelong library users.

REFERENCES

American Association of School Librarians/Association for Educational Communications and Technology. 1998. *Information Power: Building Partnerships for Learning*. Chicago: American Library Association.

Anderson, S. B. 2005. *Extreme Teens: Library Services to Nontraditional Young Adults*. Westport, CT: Libraries Unlimited.

Association of College and Research Libraries. 2000. "Information Literacy Competency Standards for Higher Education." Retrieved December 18, 2008, from www.ala.org/ala/mgrps/divs/acrl/standards/informationliteracycompetency.cfm.

Association for Library and Information Science Education (ALISE). 2007. "Directory of LIS Programs and Faculty in the United States and Canada—2007." Retrieved December 18, 2008, from www.alise .org/mc/page.do?sitePageId=55644&orgId=ali.

Bernier, A., M. K. Chelton, C. A. Jenkins, and J. B. Pierce. 2005. "Two Hundred Years of Young Adult Library Services History.:" *Voice of Youth Advocates* 28:106–11.

Jenkins, C. A. 2000. "The History of Youth Services Librarianship: A Review of the Research Literature." *Libraries & Culture* 35:103–40.

Jones, P., M. Gorman, and T. Suellentrop. 2004. *Connecting Young Adults and Libraries: A How-to-Do-It Manual for Librarians.* 3rd ed. New York: Neal-Schuman.

U.S. Census Bureau. 2008. "Resident Population by Age and Sex. The 2009 Statistical Abstract." Retrieved on December 18. 2008, from www.census.gov/compendia/statab/cats/population/estimates_and_ projections_by_age_sex_raceethnicity.html.

Young Adult Library Services Association (YALSA). 2003. "Young Adults Deserve the Best: Competencies for Librarians Serving Young Adults." Retrieved on December 18, 2008, from www.ala.org/ala/ mgrps/divs/yalsa/profdev/yacompetencies/competencies.cfm.

Young Adult Library Services Association (YALSA). n.d. "Who Was Mike Printz?" Retrieved on December 18, 2008, from www.ala.org/ala/mgrps/divs/yalsa/booklistsawards/printzaward/ whowasmikeprintz/whomikeprintz.cfm.

Issue Paper 1
The Importance of a Whole Library Approach to Public Library Young Adult Services: A YALSA Issue Paper

Written for YALSA by Linda W. Braun with contributions from Sarah Flowers and Mary Hastler

Adopted by YALSA's Board of Directors, January 8, 2011

Introduction

It is crucial that the all library staff have the skills and knowledge necessary to serve the young adult population with respect and first-rate services. When all public libraries are fully staffed only with those that value young adults, not only does the library thrive, but the community, of which adolescents are a part, thrives as well.

When an adolescent walks into a library he or she may use any number of the services available. A 17-year-old customer may visit the library's technology center in order to locate information about jobs that are available after graduation from high school. A 15-year-old student might seek help from reference staff to complete a research paper on the causes of the French revolution. It is essential that these young adults receive the information-seeking assistance required from well-trained and respectful staff. When they do, the library provides the value that the community deserves.

Abstract

Any community member that walks into a public library or visits a library website should expect the highest quality of service available. This is no truer for children than it is for adults, and no truer for adults than it is for young adults. In some communities, teens are relegated to a specific area of the library with the hope that they will stay there, and that the one staff member assigned to work with teens will keep anyone in that age group out of the way of everyone else. Appropriate and attractive space for teens to read, do homework, and socialize is important but teens also need to feel welcome in all areas of the library.

It is important when promoting positive adolescent development for teens that the age-group be treated equitably—and teens know when there is a service double standard in place. As a result, teens sometimes choose to exhibit undesirable behaviors or choose to no longer use the institution that they perceive as treating them inappropriately. The ramifications on the library can be long term as support from future taxpayers is potentially lost. Teens may also fight back with displays of inappropriate behavior while in the library and these can extend into the local community.

Adolescence is a confusing time for many teens and as a result it is also turbulent for those around them. Young adults are grown but not fully grown. Teenagers can act like adults one minute and like children the next. It's sometimes hard to know what to expect, which is one of the reasons why many adults are wary around the age group.

This dynamic does not have to exist and it can be changed by providing young adults in the library with a full-complement of services and staff who have the skills and knowledge necessary to serve the age group. This can be accomplished through staff professional development, collaboration, and administrative support.

Problem Statement

Young adult service staffing models in public libraries across the United States vary widely. Examples include libraries with:

- no staff members assigned responsibilities that focus on services to adolescents
- staff with primary responsibilities in children's or adult areas that are also asked to provide services to teens on an ad hoc basis
- a staff member that is designated as a part-time teen services librarian while also responsible for at least one other area of library services to a different population group.
- a staff member that is a designated full-time teen services librarian
- staff that make up a full teen department with full-time and part-time members directly (and only) assigned to serving teens.

The ideal in any library is to have at least one full-time young adult librarian and to have all staff throughout the library fully understand the developmental needs of young adults and possess the skills necessary to serve teens successfully. This ideal has proved hard to achieve. In their 2007 study, the Public Library Association found that only 51 percent of public libraries have a full-time young adults services librarian. Sixty-two percent of these libraries have at least one staff person whose job it is specifically to serve teens. This is an improvement over figures from 1994, which indicated that only 11 percent of public libraries had a staff person whose job it was to serve teens. Still, there is plenty of room for improvement.

Many libraries have staff in non-teen departments that are wary of adolescents and/or choose to have nothing to do with the age group. In many of these libraries administration, for whatever reason, does not stand up for teenagers as a unique age group and require that all staff provide the age group with high-quality service.

Recognizing that not all teen services specialists (along with library staff members who are not teen services specialists but yet interact with teens on a regular basis) are able to keep up with teen-related research and skills, in 1996 YALSA launched the Serving the Underserved program. This initiative provided train-the-trainer professional development to librarians across the United States. This training enabled trainees to take their learning back into their own communities and assist colleagues and peers in providing better service to adolescents. Overall, the program laid the groundwork for supporting staff not specifically trained to work with young adults so that all library staff members could serve the age group successfully.

At the time that YALSA initiated the Serving the Underserved program, libraries around the country started to recognize the importance of teen services. This acknowledgment is seen in the growth of YALSA, which in the mid-to-late 2000s saw strong increases in membership and this growth led to the Association's becoming the fastest growing division of the American Library Association (ALA).

A factor leading to the increased recognition of young adults in libraries was the sheer number of teenagers in the United States. Census figures released in 2008 show that there were close to 42 million young adults in the U.S. This large number of adolescents, along with the burgeoning of social media use by teens, the surge in the quantity of information available to young adults in print and on the web, and the significant growth of publishing in young adult literature, led to acknowledgment by some librarians that young adults require a full complement of high-quality library services in order to support their use of and access to a variety of technologies and print resources.

Research on teens and their developmental needs and behaviors is a growing field as researchers seek data on the impact on new technologies on the teenage brain. In November 2010, Harvard researcher, Dr. Frances Jensen, spoke to neuroscientists about scientific findings that demonstrate the brain is only 80 percent developed when a child reaches adolescence (Juskalian, 2010). These findings are an important part of this discussion because they point to the need for librarians to not make assumptions about young adult abilities and knowledge. While teens have brains that are more developed than those of children, young adults don't have the brain of a fully developed adult. As a result, sometimes teens require support from children's services staff and sometimes they require support from those primarily tasked with serving adults. And, there are times when a young adult services librarian is exactly what an adolescent needs. Adolescents are grown but not fully grown and as such need to have library services that support their needs as developing adults who must make use of children's, young adult, and adult library programs and services.

Proposed Solution

In 2010 YALSA updated its Competencies for Librarians Serving Youth: Young Adults Deserve the Best and added a companion book and evaluation tool to the suite of competency materials available. This update and expansion increased the number of resources available that aid state level library agency staff, administrators, and front-line librarians in development of high-quality teen library services and the evaluation and measurement of these services. The Communication, Marketing, and Outreach section of the competencies states, "The librarian will be able to establish an environment in the library wherein all staff serve young adults with courtesy and respect, and all staff are encouraged to promote programs and services for young adults." This statement highlights the value of providing young adult services outside of the isolated framework of a sole teen librarian being the only staff member that is knowledgeable about, and providing services to, the age group.

Anyone spending time in a public library will quickly see how frequently young adults use all aspects of library services. For example, teens:

- Repeatedly require assistance and support from reference staff to locate homework materials and materials that support personal information needs.

- Need to discuss borrowing records with circulation staff.
- Use computers and other technologies for reading, writing, communicating, collaborating, and creating and often need the support of information technology staff as they work on projects in these areas.
- Take part in events and programs sponsored by agencies with which library outreach staff collaborates.
- Spend time in the children's, teen, and adult departments in order to locate materials or to help out with programs.

How can all library staff support young adults that use a wide variety of library spaces and resources?

STAFF TRAINING AND PROFESSIONAL DEVELOPMENT

A library with a strong commitment to young adults guarantees that the age group is treated with respect by the entire library staff. This is possible only when all staff take part in training related to the developmental assets of teens. Knowledge of these assets, and of why they are important to the successful growth of adolescents, provides library staff with a foundation from which to work when developing policies, collections and programs. This knowledge also provides an understanding of why teens behave as they do when inside a library as well as a comprehension of how to react to sometimes challenging young adult behaviors.

COLLABORATION IN COLLECTION DEVELOPMENT

Young adult services staff, reference staff and children's services staff must work together to plan for collections that not only support the homework help needs of young adults, but also meet the personal information needs of the age group. Both male and female adolescents require opportunities to access materials such as those that support their personal interests from learning about relationships, to discovering options for life after high school, to finding out about current trends in entertainment or fashion. A full complement of materials such as magazines and books in the adult, teen, and children's areas of the library are required in order to support the educational, recreational and personal growth needs of teens at all levels of development.

INFORMATION LITERACY SUPPORT ACROSS LIBRARY DEPARTMENTS

Data released by the Pew Internet and American Life Project in February 2010 found that "Teens continue to be avid users of social networking websites—as of September 2009, 73% of online American teens ages 12 to 17 used an online social network website, a statistic that has continued to climb upwards from 55% in November 2006 and 65% in February 2008." (Pew, 2010) This high rate of young adult use of virtual social networking points to the need for technology, reference, and teen services staff to work together to develop face-to-face and virtual programs that support teens' information literacy needs and their need to learn to be safe and smart when communicating and collaborating in virtual environments.

PROGRAMMING FOR PARENTS REGARDING ADOLESCENCE AND ADOLESCENT TRENDS

Technology, adult services, children's services, and teen services staff also play a part in educating parents, teachers, and others about the role technology plays in the lives of teens. Many adults that live and work with teens do not have a firm understanding of the why and how of teen technology use, particularly use related to social media and interactive technologies (often referred to as Web 2.0). Education by librarians on this topic helps adults better understand young adult interests and behaviors within the social media arena.

Similarly, parents are not always secure in their understanding of the changes that take place as their children move from childhood to adulthood. Parents may feel comfortable with children's staff after years of bringing their children to programs at the library and these staff can help a parent with learning how to live with a teen. Adult staff may have a rapport with parents with whom they discuss fiction and nonfiction materials checked out of the library. Due to this rapport, these staff members may prove to be the best qualified to help parents find resources that help them to understand the changes a teenage son or daughter is experiencing.

CROSS-GENERATIONAL MENTORING OPPORTUNITIES

Children's services, adult services, and young adult services staff that work together to plan initiatives that provide teens with opportunities to mentor children and tutor seniors play a significant role in helping young adults gain important developmental assets. The Search Institute's list of assets that teens need in order to grow-up successfully includes assets of empowerment, support, and social competencies. Programs in which teens share skills and knowledge with those younger and older are essential in helping teens to gain these assets and therefore play a role in an adolescent's long-term growth and development.

Future Directions

Success in the whole library approach to young adult services will occur with complete support from library administration. Administrators that move forward in this framework will:

- Model for all staff members high-quality librarian and young adult customer service interactions. Not only will these interactions serve as models for staff, they will also demonstrate the administrator's own understanding of teen developmental assets and needs.
- Regularly provide opportunities for all library staff to take part in professional development focusing on techniques for working with adolescents. Continuing education will also be made available on topics related teen trends in areas including technology, popular culture, information, and social experiences and behaviors.
- Regularly evaluate library services looking specifically at the quality of teen services across all library departments and communicate with staff to inform them when instances of inadequate service to young adults occur. The administrator will also inform staff that such service is not acceptable in the library.
- Hire only staff that is able to demonstrate the ability to work with young adults no matter what library department is designated as his or her main service area.
- Speak out to community and government agencies, parents, and staff on the value of young adults in the library and in the community as a whole.

Recommendations

The Young Adult Library Services Association asserts that young adult services must be integrated into public libraries as a part of a full continuum of library service. Because adolescents require library services that support unique developmental needs both at the upper and lower ends of the age spectrum, it is crucial that libraries and library staff embrace a whole library approach and integrate teen services into the entire library program including children's, young adult, adult, reference, circulation, technology, and technical services.

RESOURCES

Flowers, Sarah. *Young Adults Deserve the Best: YALSA's Competencies in Action.* ALA, 2010.

Juskalian, Russ. "The Kids Can't Help It," *Newsweek,* Dec. 16, 2010. www.newsweek.com/2010/12/16/the-kids-can-t-help-it.html.

Pew Internet in American Life Project. "Social Media & Young Adults: Social Media," Feb. 3, 2010, www.pewinternet.org/Reports/2010/ Social-Media-and-Young-Adults/Part-3/1-Teens-and-online-social-networks.aspx.

Public Library Association. *2007 PLDS Statistical Report.* Chicago: PLA, 2007.

Search Institute. "40 Developmental Assets for Adolescents 12 to 18." (2007). http://www.search-institute.org/content/40-developmental-assets-adolescents-ages-12-18.

U. S. Census Bureau. "Resident Population by Age and Sex: The 2009 Statistical Abstract," 2008, www.census.gov/compendia/statab/cats/ population/estimates_and_projections_by_age_sex_raceethnicity.html

YALSA with Audra Caplan, "The Benefits of Including Dedicated Young Adult Librarians on Staff in the Public Library," January 2009, www.ala.org/ala/mgrps/divs/yalsa/profdev/whitepapers/yastaff.cfm

YALSA. "YALSA's Competencies for Librarians Serving Youth: Young Adults Deserve the Best," January 2010, www.ala.org/yalsa/ competencies.